MURDEROUS MINDS FRANCE

MURDEROUS MINDS FRANCE
International Serial Killers Encyclopedia
Book 3

ALAN R. WARREN

House of Mystery Publishing

Seattle, Washington, USA

Vancouver, British Columbia, Canada

First Edition

ISBN (Paperback): 978-1-989980-91-0
ISBN (eBook): 978-1-989980-90-3

Cover design, formatting, layout, and editing by Evening Sky Publishing Services

Contents

Book Description

Step into the abyss with this gripping series that unravels the chilling tales of serial killers worldwide. From the damp and foggy streets of Victorian London to the bustling metropolises of modern-day America, no corner of the globe is left unexplored. Each book in the series delves into a different region, offering a comprehensive look at the infamous serial killers who have left a trail of terror in their wake.

The *International Serial Killers Encyclopedia* series sheds light on the murderous minds of many killers, including their motivations, methods, and madness, through detailed research and explicit retelling of events. Some are notorious names that echo through history books, while others are lesser-known killers whose stories are no less harrowing. Each volume reveals a new layer of darkness.

Amidst the horror, there are tales of resilience and justice – the strength of survivors and the justice meted out by the tireless efforts of law enforcement. These stories are a compelling blend of true crime facts and psychological insight and a haunting journey through the twisted minds and deeds of serial killers from around the world. Prepare to be enthralled, horrified, and captivated as you delve into the shadows of the abyss.

Monstrous Minds France takes you deep into the twisted psyches of France's most notorious serial killers. From the grisly scenes of their crimes to the psychological profiles that unravel their motives, this book offers a chilling exploration of evil incarnate. Each chapter unveils a new horror story, detailing the lives, deeds, and capture of these monstrous individuals who left a trail of fear across the French landscape. Through meticulous research and compelling narratives, *Monstrous*

Minds France sheds light on the darkness within, leaving readers haunted by the complex web of human depravity and the enduring quest for justice.

Introduction

Welcome to the third volume of the *International Serial Killers Encyclopedia* series, *Murderous Minds: France*. This edition delves deep into France's dark history, uncovering the sinister stories of its most notorious serial killers. From the cobblestone streets of Paris to the quiet countryside, this volume explores the chilling tales of those who have terrorized the nation with their heinous acts.

France, a country renowned for its rich culture, exquisite cuisine, and historical landmarks, also harbors a darker, more sinister side. In *Murderous Minds: France*, we journey into the shadowy world of French serial killers, examining the lives and crimes of those who have left an indelible mark on the nation's history.

This volume provides an in-depth exploration of some of France's most infamous murderers, uncovering the psychological complexities and motivations that drove them to commit their atrocities. Through meticulous research and compelling storytelling, we reveal the chilling details of their crimes, the investigations that led to their capture, and the trials that brought them to justice.

Murderous Minds: France is a gripping and informative addition to the *International Serial Killers Encyclopedia* series, that is perfect for true crime enthusiasts, researchers, and anyone with a fascination for the macabre aspects of human nature. Prepare to be captivated by the haunting and disturbing stories that reveal the darkest depths of the French criminal underworld.

ONE

Joseph Vacher

THE FRENCH RIPPER

J oseph Gleydson Vacher was born in Beaufort, Isere, France, in 1869. There are no records of the exact date or place that he was born, but he was one of fifteen children in the family. His father was uneducated but a strict disciplinarian who sent Joseph to Catholic school. At about twenty-two, he joined the army in 1892 to escape his poor and strict family life. It was believed that one of the reasons Joseph joined the military was to impress a woman, Louise, whom he had met and fallen in love with. She never returned his affection, though, no matter what he did to try and impress her.

While he was serving in the army, Vacher attempted to commit suicide on two different occasions by cutting his own throat. He claimed he did this because his commanding officers had not given him the proper recognition that he felt he deserved. Vacher seemed to have an inflated view of his importance in his unit and thought he should be promoted. After his second attempt to kill himself, he was dismissed from the army.

Once out, he spent all his time trying to win over Louise. He asked her to marry him, but she refused. On one occasion, Louise made fun of his attempts to marry her, and Joseph responded with great anger. He was about to attack her physically, but he managed to stop himself from doing it. Louise laughed at him out loud again, and Vacher snapped. He went and got his gun, came back, and shot her four times, then himself. Both survived their wounds.

Vacher's wounds from shooting himself in the head left his face partially paralyzed. It made people who met him think his face was deformed. One of the bullets the doctors were not able to remove stayed lodged in his ear for the rest of his life. The way people reacted to his facial injury created a deep anger that he could not overcome. After the murder-suicide attempt on Louise, he was placed in a mental institute located in Dole, Jura, for one year. After a year, the doctors declared him cured and released him in 1894 when he was twenty-five.

Not long after Vacher was released from the mental institute, he began a series of murders that lasted three years. During these years, he killed at least eleven people, including one woman, five teenage boys, and five teenage boys. His victims were all shepherds he found while watching their flocks in an isolated field with nobody else around.

At this time, Vacher had no home and lived on the streets, traveling around without any direction. Going from town to town, he usually found that the farmers would give him small jobs to earn money or food. While in the city, he would not look for work, opting instead to beg on the streets.

In 1897, Vacher's murder spree would come to an end. After seeing a woman gathering wood in a field located near Ardeche, he attacked her. She screamed and fought back. Her husband and son were not far away, and when they heard her yelling, they came running to her. They stopped the attack and took Vacher to the police station.

While police were interviewing Vacher about attacking the woman, he ended up confessing to the other eleven murders he had committed. At the time, police had no idea that Vacher was involved in the other murders. They weren't even looking at him as a suspect.

Vacher was able to not only tell them about who he murdered and where he murdered them but also what he did to them during the attack. All of his victims had been sexually assaulted, including the boys, disemboweled, and stabbed to death. He exhibited a real sense of anger while describing the murders.

Once Vacher was charged with his crimes, he tried to say that he was innocent because he was insane at the time of the murders. He first told investigators that a rabid dog had bitten him and given him blood poisoning, causing him to go insane. Then, he said that God had sent him, and he was supposed to be committing the murders. He claimed that God wanted him to murder these people as they were doing the devil's work.

Police sent Vacher for a psychiatric evaluation, which determined that he was fit to stand trial.

On October 28, 1898, Vacher was tried and convicted at the Assie Court and sentenced to the death penalty. Two months later, at dawn on December 31, 1898, Vacher was executed by guillotine. During the execution, Vacher refused to move and had to be carried up to the guillotine.

TWO

Jeanne Weber

THE OGRESS

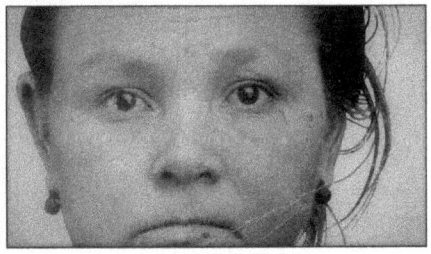

Not much is known about Jeanne Weber's early years except that she was born on the coast of western France on October 7, 1874. She left the town and went to Paris when she was fourteen. She worked whatever kind of jobs she could get. Most of them were menial cleaning jobs, and all of them were temporary.

When she turned nineteen years old in 1893,

she married a man who was a laborer and a bad alcoholic. They lived in a poor part of town and had three children. She began babysitting for neighbors, different family members, and friends to make extra money. Jeanne had started drinking as much as her husband.

In 1905, two of Jeanne's children became sick and died, but neither she nor her husband seemed upset by this happening. They didn't have a funeral service and hardly told anyone. Their only remaining child was a seven-year-old boy, who later died as well.

On March 2, 1905, while Jeanne was babysitting her sister-in-law's two daughters, eighteen-month-old Georgette became sick. Jeanne did nothing about it. Later that night, Georgette died. Nobody noticed anything strange at the time, including their family doctor.

Almost two weeks later, on March 11th, Jeanne was asked to babysit for her sister-in-law again. This time, their two-year-old daughter, Suzanne, died from what Jeanne said were convulsions. The family doctor backed up her claim.

Two weeks later, on March 25th, Jeanne was babysitting her brother's daughter, Germaine, who was seven years old. During the night, Germain began to choke so severely that she had red marks on her throat. But she recovered.

The following night, Jeanne returned to babysit her niece again while her brother went to work. Germaine had another coughing and choking fit, but this time, she died. The doctor told the family that Germaine probably had diphtheria.

Jeanne returned to her brother's house four nights later to babysit his three-year-old son, Marcel. He, too, died that night with the same symptoms his sister had: choking and coughing. Again, his death would be blamed on diphtheria, even though both children had bruises and marks all over their necks.

Jeanne's remaining child also died in March.

The following month, on April 5th, Jeanne invited her two sisters-in-law for dinner. They went shopping afterward and left their children with Jeanne. When the two women returned to Jeanne's house a little earlier than expected, they found ten-year-old Maurice lying on a bed, bruised, beaten, and grasping for air. Jeanne was caught red-handed, standing over him with an angry expression and screaming at him. Police were called, and charges were laid against Jeanne.

By the time the trial began on January 29,

1906, the prosecutor had charged Jeanne with eight murders, and her own three children who died were among them. The famous and brilliant defence lawyer, Henri Robert, was her attorney. He always took cases the media reported about often since it meant his name would also be in the papers.

On February 6th, the jury acquitted Jeanne because they couldn't believe a nice girl like her could murder all of those children.

In the Spring of the following year, on April 7, 1907, in Villedieu, a servant went to the local doctor's office and asked that he check on a sick boy. When the doctor arrived at the house, nine-year-old Auguste was lying dead in his bed. He had several bruises and marks on his neck and face, and the babysitter, Madame Moulinet, told the doctor that the boy was having fits and coughing. So, the doctor listed the cause of death as convulsions.

A month later, on May 4th, the doctor changed his mind on the cause of death, claiming that the boy had been murdered once he found out that the babysitter's real name was Jeanne Weber.

Weber was charged with the boy's death, and she again asked the lawyer, Henri Roberts, to take the case. The trial date was set, but once the second autopsy report came back stating that the boy had died of typhoid, she was released.

After this, Jeanne Weber worked as an orderly at a children's hospital in Faucombault. Then, she worked for some old friends who owned a children's home in Orangeville. Jeanne changed her name to Marie Lemoine to hide from the public and to avoid harassment. Only her friends knew who she was. They believed in her innocence and that the police did her wrong.

Within a week of Jeanne being at home, she was caught trying to strangle one of the boys at the house. The owners fired her but didn't report thc incident to the police.

Jeanne next appeared in Paris, where she was homeless and walking the streets. She was arrested for vagrancy and placed in an asylum, where they diagnosed her as sane and released her. She then began to prostitute to make money. She moved into a cheap hotel with a man she was dating.

The owner of the hotel came home one day to find Jeanne in his home, strangling his ten-year-old son. Jeanne had to be punched in the face three times before she would let go of the dead boy. She was arrested and charged with murder.

After a medical examination, she was declared

insane. On October 25, 1908, Jeanne Weber was placed in an asylum in Mareville, where she lived for ten years before committing suicide in 1918.

The court had assigned Jeanne Weber responsible for the death of ten children.

THREE

Francois Tomasini

F rancois Cecco Tomasini was born in Venzolasca in 1880. The exact date and location is unknown. Not much is known about his childhood or family either, except that he had at least three brothers.

As a teenager, Francois was regularly in trouble with the police for minor crimes and small thefts. By the time he was twenty-seven years old, he had ten convictions for more significant thefts, robberies, as well as assault and battery.

In 1907, Francois started working as a laborer in a commune, Haute-Corse, in Corsica. There, he met a woman and got married. In December of that year, Francois argued with another laborer at the camp, which turned physical. The man he fought with died from his injuries. He was arrested, convicted of manslaughter, and sentenced to five years in prison. He was also banned from returning to the town of Haute-Corse for ten years.

When Francois was released after serving his sentence, he ignored the court-ordered ban and moved back to Haute-Corse, Corsica. To keep a low profile, he avoided the local bars and restaurants and traveled to neighboring villages.

On November 11, 1913, Francois went to a bar with some of his friends in Volpajola. While drinking at the bar, he noticed an older man, Raffaeli, who had an accordion. Thinking it would be fun, he asked the man if he and his friends could use Raffaeli's accordion and sing a song. Raffaeli's wife, the owner of the accordion, had recently died, so the seventy-nine-year-old farmer said no to Francois.

Francois became angry and started yelling at Raffaeli. He slapped him in the face before Raeffaeli's friend, Roch Sarti, stood up and told Francois to leave him alone. Francois pulled out his gun and shot Sarti twice. One bullet went through his heart, killing him immediately, and the second hit his arm.

Francois fled from the bar. For some reason,

he went to Sarti's home, where he attacked Sarti's daughter and shot Felix Gabrielli, a twenty-seven-year-old man staying at the house, in the head twice, killing him as well.

Francois then disappeared and went into hiding. The police put out a warrant for his arrest and began a search for him. Francois wasn't arrested for a couple of months when police finally found him in Luciana on January 11, 1914. He had been living with another man, Ange-Paul Giorgetti, who was also arrested and charged with harboring a fugitive. Francois was charged with two murders.

During his trial, Francois claimed that he shot Sarti in self-defense. But after all the witnesses testified against him, he was found guilty on both charges. On July 26, 1914, Francois was sentenced to death. He was taken to the prison in Bastia and executed on December 23, 1914.

FOUR

Pierre Lagrée

L'AMERICAIN

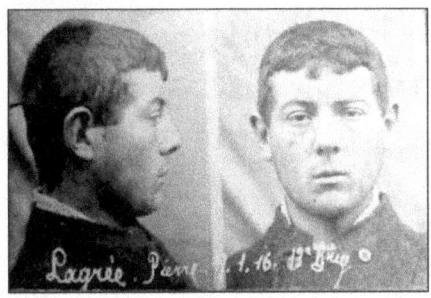

Pierre-Marie Lagrée was born in Quessoy, France, on November 20, 1896. He was one of two sons of a baker. His father often disciplined Pierre for many things, primarily fighting with his brother or lying to the family. At seven years old, Pierre started stealing from people. Small things initially that often weren't noticed. By the time he reached the age of twelve, his thefts had become much more significant, and he would frequently get caught. Pierre ran away from home at fifteen because he couldn't handle living with his father's rules. He went to Saint-Malo, where he got a job working on a ship headed to Newfoundland, Canada.

Pierre didn't like working on the ship as much as he thought he would. He couldn't handle the hard labor and was laughed at by the other crew members. Pierre quit that ship and decided to see if things would work better on a different boat. He tried two other vessels in the following two months, but neither worked out.

After Pierre quit his last job, he had enough money to catch a train to Buffalo, New York, in America. He worked as a porter in a hotel there and did well. Eventually, he went to Arcade in New York and became a farmhand with the money he had saved from his job.

It was 1914, and World War I started. During the next few months, his mother would send Pierre letters daily, begging him to come home to fight for France. After a few months, he finally agreed to return home to his mother in Quessoy. When he arrived home, everyone started calling him "American." They said he had an American accent, even when speaking French.

Soon after, Pierre enlisted in the military and became an infantryman in the First Colonial Infantry Division. He didn't like that his new salary was only thirty-five francs and complained to his mother, asking her for some extra money so that he could buy things, but she said no. So, he started stealing it. If somebody caught him or tried to stop him, he killed them.

In the Fall of 1914, Pierre was stationed in the north of France at Tot-de-Bas, where he had to bunk with Edouard Bitel, a twenty-one-year-old private who worked as a clockmaker before the war. Bitel always wore a small bag tied around his neck. In that bag, he carried any valuables or things of importance, like a picture or rings from someone he cared about.

On December 1, 1915, the two bunkmates decided to drink at a bar. Later that night, they left the bar and headed back to the base, walking through a field. Halfway through the field, Pierre hit Bitel with a beer bottle over his head, and Bitel fell to the ground. Bitel rolled around and tried to stand. But Pierre grabbed a heavy stick and hit him over the head again, killing Bitel. Pierre ripped the bag of valuables from Bitel's neck and returned to the base alone.

It was two days before Bitel's body was found

by the local police. They conducted a medical examination of his body and determined that blunt-force trauma to the head killed him. Investigators figured that Bitel was probably first hit with a bottle because there were pieces of glass and cuts on his head. They thought that he was probably killed by another soldier who was out drinking with him one night and also thought that whoever it was might have some cuts on their hands from the broken bottle.

The same day that Bitel's body was recovered, Pierre applied for leave. It was granted, and he went back home for a while. Shortly after he was gone, the police examined all the soldiers' hands to look for any cuts on them. But Pierre was already gone.

Back home in Quessoy, he visited Bitel's family, telling them they had been good friends. He even offered to be a pallbearer at their son's funeral. At the funeral, he acted strangely and promised Bitel's parents that he would find and take care of their son's murderer.

On January 3, 1916, he decided that he was going to rob the house of a woman he knew, Mrs. Monvieux. She was at home cooking dinner for her two children, an eight-year-old daughter named Marie and a four-year-old son, Joseph.

When he got there, he knocked at the front door. Knowing him, she let him in, and the two began to quarrel. After a short time, she slapped him across the face, and he responded by hitting her with his fists. He beat her so severely that she died from her injuries.

Then, he noticed both children standing and watching the horrifying scene. He pulled out a knife he was carrying and began to chase them. Pierre caught both of them and slit their throats. He quickly went through the house, looking for what he could rob, but only found fifty francs. He washed the blood from his hands and fled.

The gruesome crime scene was discovered the next day, and police were notified. When investigators started questioning the neighbors, they learned that a few had seen Pierre leaving the house the night before. Knowing his criminal history, they arrested him and brought him in for questioning.

During the police interview, they noticed several scratch marks on Pierre's face and hands, as well as what looked like blood stains on his clothing. He was put in a jail cell while the police decided whether they should charge him or if it should be the military court that should. While he was in jail waiting for the decision to be made, all of the neighbors and newspapers began accusing him of also killing Bitel.

Pierre admitted to having killed Mrs. Monvieux and her two children but said he knew nothing about the Bitel murder. He said that he only murdered Monvieux for her money and that he regretted having to kill her children.

On April 16, 1916, it was decided that the military court should try him, and he was sent to the prison in Rennes, where his trial was scheduled for July 25th. About one week before the trial began, Pierre tried to escape by surprising the guards watching him. During the struggle, Pierre stabbed one of the guards in the stomach with his bayonet. The noise of the fight and screams alerted other guards, who soon came and subdued Pierre. The two guards he injured both recovered, but the court added two attempted murder charges to the list.

In the trial, Pierre was able to describe the murders he committed while remaining very calm and rational. His relaxed demeanor led the court to give him a psychiatric exam to make sure that he was fit to continue the trial. It was determined that he was aware of right or wrong and was sane enough for a trial.

Pierre was found guilty of four counts of

murder, two counts of attempted murder, and two counts of theft. He was sentenced to death.

Pierre Lagrée was executed on August 21, 1916, by firing squad at the Rennes Military Prison, where more than one hundred people were allowed to attend. Before he was executed, he confessed to having murdered two other people while he was living in Buffalo, New York.

FIVE

Henri Désiré Landru

THE BLUEBEARD OF GAMBAIS

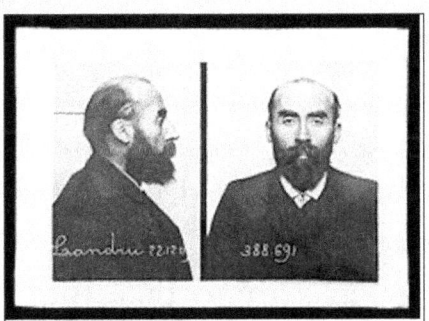

H enri Désiré Landru was born in Paris, France, on April 12, 1869. He was the youngest of two children. His father was a furnace stoker, and his mother worked in a laundry. The family was strict, devout Catholics, and Henri was educated at a Catholic school on the Ile Saint-Louis. He was also an altar boy at his parent's church.

When he turned sixteen, the church promoted him to Sub-Deacon, responsible for lighting candles and helping the priest with vestments. He met his future wife, Marie-Catherine, during a Sunday Mass in 1887. After Landru started his three years of mandatory military service in 1891, Marie-Catherine had their first child. They were unmarried, which was a scandal among their families and the town. Landru returned from service in the Fall of 1893, and the couple married. They would have four children.

Landru had problems keeping a job longer than a few months at a time. He did everything from working as a plumber and furniture salesman to being a toy maker's assistant. Throughout this time, he dreamed of becoming a great inventor, which led to trouble for him. In 1989, he designed a motorbike that he called the "Landru." He began selling his idea to investors to build a production factory to make and sell this bike. He received enough money to follow his dream but ended up running away with the money instead.

Landru went to different cities and lived off the money he had scammed from investors. Knowing that he would eventually need more money, he devised a new invention in each town he went to and sold it to investors there. Once he reeled them in, he took their money and left for another city. Some of the other plans he devised were the design of a suburban railway for Paris and an automatic toy for children.

In 1904, the police finally caught up with Landru and arrested him. He only visited his family in Paris once or twice yearly to avoid being caught. During one visit with his family, he attempted to commit fraud at a bank. One of their managers caught him, and he ran out of the building and down the street. While he was running, he tripped, fell, and hurt himself to the point where he couldn't walk. The police came, and after they realized who he was, they arrested him.

Landru attempted to kill himself during his first night in jail by wrapping his bed sheet around his neck. But one of the guards saw him and stopped him. They gave him a psychiatric exam where he was diagnosed as being close to madness but not fully and, therefore, responsible for his actions. Landru was tried and convicted of fraud. He was sentenced to two years in prison.

Over the next ten years, Landru was in and out of prison. Each time he got out, he was soon arrested again for another fraud he had committed and jailed again for a few years. All this time, his wife and four children had to fend for themselves and live in cheaper, run-down rental apartments, often in the worst parts of Paris.

In 1909, Landru met an elderly widow from Lille. He pretended to be a wealthy businessman and was caught trying to scam her out of her investments. He was charged again and sentenced to three years in prison. While he was in jail this time, his father hanged himself. Landru's wife claimed his father did it because of the shame his son brought to him.

Once released in 1912, Landru returned home to his wife, and according to her, he stole the 12,000 francs that his father had bequeathed her and the four children when he died.

In the Fall of 1913 and the Winter of 1914, Landru made plans to build an automobile factory and started selling the idea to investors. Again, he never intended to create such a factory. He collected 35,650 francs and disappeared in April 1914 with all the investment money. Later that Summer, he was tried and convicted of fraud in absentia and sentenced to serve four years of hard labor in prison the next time he was caught. In addition to the hard labor, after finishing the hard labor, he was to be exiled to the French Pacific Islands for the rest of his life.

When Landru ran away with the investment money this last time in 1914, he went to the village of Chantilly, located about fifty kilometers north of Paris. He met and became involved with a widower, Jeanne Cuchut, a thirty-nine-year-old seamstress who had lived alone for the last five years. Landru told her that his name was Raymond Diard, that he was from the northern part of France, and that he was a wealthy industrialist. He talked her into selling her dress shop and marrying him. She did, believing that he would take care of her from now on.

Cuchut returned to Paris in early August, and Landru was supposed to meet her there, but he never showed up. She moved in with her son, who had an apartment there. Since Germany had just declared war with France, she was worried. So later that year, Cuchut, her son, and brother-in-law returned to her Chantilly apartment, hoping to find Landru there. Instead, she found Landru's identification and finally discovered he was a criminal who was supposed to be exiled. The three of them returned to Paris.

Cuchut was understandably upset and told her family that the relationship with Landru was over.

Shortly after that, Landru reappeared. Somehow, he convinced her to resume their relationship and moved in with her. Landru was now calling himself Monsieur Cuchut, and along with her son, the three of them moved into a house in Vernouillet, about thirty-five kilometers away from Paris.

As Christmas neared, Cuchut's family members and friends wrote to her, intending to get together over the holiday. Cuchut replied, telling them it was not good weather where they were now living and, thus, not a good time to visit. By the new year, Cuchut and her son disappeared without a trace and were never seen again. It was suspected Landru killed them both.

Landru not only continued to defraud many people out of money, but he also committed at least nine more murders over the next four years. All his victims lived in Paris.

Forty-six-year-old Therese Laborde-Line was a widow living alone. She had also been estranged from her son and daughter-in-law and lived alone. She met Landru through an ad in the Lonely Hearts section of the *Journal Newspaper*. She went missing in June 2015.

Fifty-two-year-old Marie-Angelique Guillen was a widowed, retired housekeeper living in the

Gare de Lyon. She also answered Landru's ad that he had placed in the Lonely Hearts section of the newspaper. Once he learned about her large inheritance from her last employer, he pretended to be the Consulate General of Australia. He needed a wife to host all the diplomats he had to entertain. She disappeared in August 2015.

Fifty-five-year-old Berthe Heon was a retired cleaning woman who lived alone after losing her husband and three children. She met Landru through the Lonely Hearts ad that he had placed in the newspaper in the Summer of 2015. Landru had pretended to be a businessman going to Tunisia and needed a wife there to help start his new developments. Heon was last seen in December 1915.

Forty-four-year-old Anna Collomb was a typist for an insurance company. After her husband died ten years earlier from alcoholism, their daughter was placed in the care of a nun-operated church in Italy. Collomb was searching for a proper man to marry to get her daughter back home with her. After ten years and several male lovers, none were wealthy enough for her to marry. The two met when Collomb answered Landru's Lonely Hearts ad in May 1915. She disappeared in December 1916.

The youngest victim that Landru confessed to murdering was a nineteen-year-old nanny named Andree Babelay, who, on the surface, was a nanny for a well-respected family. Behind the scenes, she was prostituting in the downtown streets of Paris. Landru picked her up, took her to a hotel room for ten days, and then moved to an apartment in the Gare du Nord part of the city. She was last seen in April 1917.

Forty-seven-year-old Celeste Buisson also answered Landru's Lonely Hearts ad in the newspaper in May 1915. Her husband had recently died, and her son had gone into battle, which made her very lonely and worried. The couple was engaged to be married during the Summer of 2015, but it would never happen, of course. Landru would leave her for months at a time during the next two years, explaining that he had to travel abroad for business. Eventually, she went missing in September 1917.

A dress shop assistant, Louise Jaume, was a divorced thirty-eight-year-old Catholic who answered Landru's Lonely Hearts ad. He told her his name was Lucien Guillet, a refugee from Ardennes, which the Germans occupied at the time. She was last seen in November 1917 when he took her to a Mass at the Basilica of Sacre Coeur in Paris.

In the meantime, Celeste Buisson's half-sister, Marie Lacoste, met Landru once during the Summer of 1915 at Buisson's apartment. At the time, Landru was using the name George Fremyet. Lacoste didn't like him when they met, often quarreling over small things. Lacoste didn't trust him and thought he might be after her sister's money. To her dismay, when Lacoste visited a couple of years later, in the Summer of 1917, she learned that her sister had turned over all her investments and bank accounts to Landru. This change caused a big fight between the two sisters as Lacoste demanded that Buisson leave Landru. But she wouldn't. After this, Lacoste never saw her sister again.

In the Fall of 1917, Lacoste started worrying about her sister. Landru was regularly sending Lacoste postcards that were supposedly coming from her sister. Lacoste became highly suspicious of the postcards as it seemed like her sister's signature kept changing. When she saw Landru, she asked him if her sister was ill because her signatures constantly changed. Landru offered to take her to their apartment, but Lacoste refused.

Her suspicion had grown to the point that she did not trust him enough to be alone with him.

Over the next year, Lacoste went on with her life, believing that her sister was too embarrassed to meet with her. Lacoste decided to forget it and stop letting it bother her.

In December 1918, Lacoste received a letter from her sister telling her that Buisson's son had lost his eyesight from an injury during battle, and she needed to borrow some money for him if she could afford to lend it. When Lacoste traveled to where Buisson had been living, she learned that she no longer lived there. The nagging dread that Landru might have done something to her sister returned.

When Lacoste returned home, she began writing a history of events, starting with when her sister first met Landru in 1915. The chronology included Landru's taking all of her sister's money and investments and Lacoste receiving fraudulently signed postcards from her sister. It also included the fact that her sister no longer lived where she used to live.

Lacoste took her notes to her local police department in Paris on January 11, 1919. The police told her she needed to take her information to the Gambais police station, where her sister disappeared.

Lacoste immediately wrote to the Mayor of Gambais and explained the situation in detail. The mayor didn't believe her. He knew the man she had described in her letter as Raoul Dupont, a respected man in the community. He didn't recognize the missing woman Lacoste described in her letter and didn't believe that she had ever lived in his town.

Undeterred, Lacoste wrote to the prosecutor's office in Gambais and explained the situation. The prosecutor filed a missing person report and sent it off to the police in Paris, who in turn called Lacoste in for an interview. She gave the detective a copy of the chronology of events she had written, which laid out her claims and evidence. The inspector took her information, leading to Landru's arrest on April 12, 1919.

But before he was arrested, thirty-seven-year-old dressmaker Anne-Marie Pascal, who made a good living making the dresses shown in different fashion houses in Paris, answered Landru's Lonely Hearts ad in September 1916. She was once married years before but had gotten a divorce after their baby died. Now that she had aged some, she told her coworkers and friends she was looking for a sugar daddy. She was last seen in April 1918.

Landru's ninth victim, whom he later confessed to investigators, was thirty-seven-year-old Marie-Therese Marchadier, who was a prostitute her whole life. She lived in an apartment on Rue Saint-Jacques, where she walked her dogs daily. Landru found her after answering her ad in the newspaper selling some of her furniture. She disappeared in January 1919.

Over these four years of killing at least nine women and committing several fraudulent scams on so many people, the main reason Landru was able to avoid detection by police was that World War I was occurring at the same time. When war broke out, the country conscripted all healthy males between the ages of ninety and thirty-five, including most working police officers in the towns. Landru lived in Gambais mainly during this period, and only one policeman was left to work in the village. The police officers left to work were usually older and even well into their seventies. They simply did not have time to focus on missing women, who were usually street workers, when the country was under attack by the Germans, and so many young men were getting killed in battle.

Landru also avoided capture because he had a lot of help from his wife and children. It became a family business. His wife played an excellent cover for him among their neighbors and friends. Their oldest son, born in 1900, helped Landru dispose of all the furniture and valuable possessions of Landru's victims in at least five cases.

During his interrogations over the next year, Landru refused to confirm his identity and insisted that he was innocent of any wrongdoing as he would never murder anyone, especially these women he insisted were his friends.

Over the following weeks, detectives gathered a lot of evidence against Landru. They had lists of assets each of his victims owned, which Landru had taken control of. They also discovered a storage place where he had kept items and even files he had created for each woman he had contact with over the years.

Police also investigated Landru's wife and children. They discovered that all were helping him in his fraudulent scamming of people but not in the murders. His son, Charles, admitted to helping his father clean out five different apartments of their possessions, all belonging to other women his father had been with.

Another son, Maurice, was arrested for

swindling investments and stealing money from women as well. Among some of the items police recovered was jewelry belonging to one of Landru's victims. In the case of the missing victim, Anna Collomb, Maurice lied about what happened to her to protect his father.

Detectives also had proof that Landru's wife had forged the signature of at least one of his victims to gain access to her bank account. She, at first, claimed that she was innocent. Later, she admitted to doing it but claimed she had no idea he was stealing from these women.

Landru was eventually charged with eleven counts of murder and brought to trial on November 7, 1921. The three-week trial in Versailles was sensationalized through the media, especially since the prosecutor and judge allowed newspapers to take pictures in the courtroom during the daily trial. His trial also attracted several French actors and celebrities to watch.

Landru had one of the country's most famous defense lawyers, Vincent de Moro Giafferri. Giafferri hated Landru with a passion but adamantly fought against the death penalty, which was the primary reason he took this case. He had a difficult time keeping Landru under control during the trial. During Landru's testimony, he told the court that he knew more about what had happened to the missing women, but he was sworn to secrecy. He claimed he made a pact with each of these women. The prosecutor had one hundred and twenty witnesses testify at the trial.

On November 30, 1921, the jury reached a verdict after only deliberating for three hours. On the eleven counts of murder, he was found guilty by nine of the jurors but not guilty by three. All twelve jurors found him guilty on all counts of theft and fraud. He was initially sentenced to death, but after an appeal, it was reduced to life imprisonment. However, the president of France, Alexandre Millerand, refused to sign the appeal, and therefore, Landru was sent back to death row to be executed.

On February 25, 1922, Landru was executed by guillotine shortly before dawn outside of the Saint-Pierre Prison in Versailles. He was buried in the Cimetiere des Gonards and Versailles. Five years after his execution, his family refused to pay for the rent on his burial plot. Oddly, in response, they dug up the grave, dismembered his remains, and buried him again in the same cemetery, only this time, it was in an unmarked grave.

In the 1930s, Landru's house in Gambais was turned into a restaurant. The owners claimed that the house was where he probably killed many of his victims, which ultimately drew large crowds. Over the years, the notoriety faded, and the restaurant closed down. The house is still there but no longer a business.

In 1923, someone bought Landru's oven in an auction. It was rumored to have been used for cooking the remains of his victims. The oven was later sent to Turin, Italy, and put on display. They charged people to come and see it. After many complaints by the French people, the city of Turin banned the ghoulish oven display, and it was taken away and bought by an unknown private collector.

SIX

Marcel Petiot

DOCTOR SATAN

M arcel André Henri Félix Petiot was
born in Auxerre, Yonne, in northern
France, on January 17, 1897. When
Petiot was fourteen, he broke into a postal box and

stole everything he could carry. Later, when he was caught, police charged him with theft and damaging the post box. During his arrest, Petiot was acting strangely, so they sent him to a doctor, who later told the court that Petoit had a mental illness. The judge dropped all the charges against Petoit, and he was allowed to return home.

When Petiot turned seventeen, he was expelled because of his persistent disturbances during classes and disrespect for the teachers. He sometimes fought with his teachers and had to be physically pulled from them. He was ordered to see a psychiatrist, and on March 14, 1914, he was again diagnosed as having a mental illness. He was then sent to a particular school for children with cognitive issues in Paris, where he graduated in the Summer of 1915.

After graduating, Petiot volunteered to join the French army in January 1916 to fight against the Germans in World War I. In April of that year, during the Second Battle of the Aisne, he was with a group of soldiers who were gassed and shot by the enemy. He was sent to various medical clinics to heal, but during his stay, he was arrested for stealing money from a wallet and morphine from the medical storage.

After that, Petiot was sent to a military prison

in Orleans, where doctors and a psychiatrist examined him. They also diagnosed him with having a mental illness. Even with his criminal history and cognitive issues, they reassigned him to the army, and he returned to battle in June 1918. Three weeks back, he hurt his foot when a grenade went off close to where he was standing. Again, he was sent to the medical unit. But this time, when he healed, he was discharged from the army and given a pension for being disabled.

After he returned home, Petiot entered the free accelerated education program the government had created for war veterans. After only eight months of medical school, he worked as an intern in a mental hospital in Evreux. After completing the necessary work hours, he achieved his medical degree in December 1921 and went to work at Villeneuve-sur-Yvonne. During his time there, he became addicted to the different drugs he took from his job. He also sold these drugs to various people who lived in the town. Petiot also performed illegal abortions.

It is believed that Petiot's first murder was an older patient's daughter, Louise Delveau, whom he had been having a secret affair with during the Spring of 1926. When she disappeared in May, and the police decided to investigate the case, they found nothing and considered her to be just a runaway. Had the detectives questioned her neighbors during their investigation, they would have discovered that Petiot had removed a large trunk from her apartment and put it into his car.

In the Summer of 1926, Petiot ran for Mayor of Villeneuve-sur-Yonne and won. During his time in office, he married the twenty-three-year-old Georgette Lablais, the daughter of a wealthy local businessman and butcher. The couple had a son in April 1928.

Several complaints started coming into the Prefect of Yonne—the person appointed by the president who is in charge of making sure that the actions of the local authorities follow the law and correctly perform their duties. The complaints were aimed at Petiot, accusing him of stealing money during financial deals he made with people for the city. In August 1931, he was suspended as Mayor and soon after resigned. His city council also resigned to show their support for Petiot.

Petiot moved back to Paris and started a medical practice there. Even though police had heard rumors that the clinic was conducting abortions and Petiot was giving out excessive prescriptions, in 1936, he was promoted to the "medicine d'etat-civil," responsible for writing the death certificates in the city.

In 1940, after France surrendered to Germany during World War II, many French citizens were used as laborers. Petiot gave fake documents to many of them, claiming that they were too sick or disabled and couldn't perform physical work for the Germans. He also treated the workers who complained of real illnesses, but because he wasn't making money from all of his work, he mainly gave people prescriptions for narcotics. In July 1942, he was caught and fined 2400 francs.

Petiot was frustrated during the German occupation because he couldn't make money or do the things that he used to do. He soon devised a scheme to make him a lot of money. Petiot would pretend that he could get people wanted by the Germans out of the country. For 25,000 francs per person, he would give safe passage to those from Portugal to Argentina.

Petiot used three different accomplices to find his victims, who were usually resistance fighters, Jews, and sometimes wealthier criminals. Once Petiot got the money he asked for, he told his victims that they needed to be vaccinated for certain things so that Argentina could let them into the country. Instead of giving them the vaccine, Petiod would inject them with cyanide and kill them. Then, he stole any valuables they had and disposed of their bodies by dumping them in the Seine River. Eventually, there started to be too many, and he was worried they might be discovered, so he began to dispose of them in a tub full of lime or by incinerating them.

In 1941, the French Gestapo, a group of French people working to help the Germans, heard about this escape route and decided to investigate. They thought it must be part of the Resistance. Three of Petiot's accomplices were arrested, and they told them about Petiot being the one who organized the whole scheme. They all spent eight months in prison for helping Jews leave the country, and Petiot was released in January 1944.

A few months later, some of Petiot's neighbors summoned the police to check his house because of the vast amounts of smoke coming from his chimney and the foul smell. Initially, the police thought it was a chimney fire, so they rushed into Petiot's house. They found a large fire burning in Petiot's stove in the basement. After they put the fire out, they found several human bones in the ashes and the basement.

Further searching of his house and property revealed a large pit dug in the backyard. Looking in it, they found more human remains covered with lime. Throughout his home and property, they found enough human remains to account for at least ten human beings. The news about this was massive and reached all parts of Europe.

A warrant was issued for the arrest of Petiot, but he was well hidden with friends who were more than willing to do anything they could to hide him. They believed that it was the Gestapo who was looking for him. While he was in hiding, France was liberated from the Germans.

Petiot changed his name to Henri Valeri and joined the French Forces of the Interior, which were part of the French Resistance. He was quickly promoted to Captain and was one of the chief interrogators of prisoners.

After a newspaper article covering the old cases that Petiot had been involved in was published, it brought back a renewal for some of the detectives who had previously searched for him. Police notified the French Forces to be on the lookout for Petiot, unaware he was a captain.

While Petiot was in the Paris Metro Station on October 31st, somebody recognized him and reported him to the police. He was arrested shortly after. At the time of his arrest, he was carrying a gun, over fifty different identifications, and over 31,000 francs.

After his arrest, Petiot was placed in the La Sante Prison. He insisted he was innocent during interrogation, claiming the only people he had ever killed were the enemies of France during the war. He also claimed that the bodies in his backyard were ones he had found in February 1944. He assumed they were collaborators of the Germans and probably killed by the Resistance.

Police were unable to find anyone who could back up Petiot's claim. He was eventually charged with twenty-seven murders for the profit of 2,000,000 francs. By the time his trial began, one hundred and thirty-five criminal charges were laid against him.

Petiot hired a famous lawyer, Rene Floriot, who often defended celebrities. Floriot argued that Petiot only murdered nineteen of the bodies found on his property and only because they were double agents and collaborators for the Germans. During the trial, his lawyer strategically referred to Petiot as a "resistance fighter for France." But this was to no avail.

The court found Petiot guilty of twenty-six murders and sentenced him to death. On May 25, 1956, Petiot was executed by guillotine and later buried in the Ivry Cemetery.

SEVEN

Giuseppe Sasia

THE SHEPHERDS' KILLER

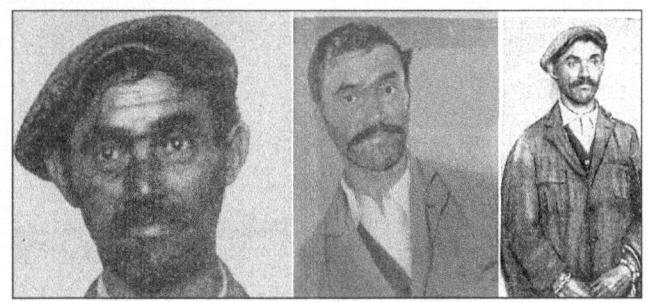

Giuseppe Sasia was born in Rossana, Piedmont, Italy, on May 26, 1886. At the age of ten, he moved to France with his family. They had farmland there, and his father had been a farmer in Italy. After his father passed away, his mother returned to her family in Italy. Giuseppe and his brother stayed in France and sold their father's farm. Later, the two brothers bought a different farm with the money they made from the sale. Later, they also sold that, and then Guiseppe purchased a restaurant in Les Acres.

Giuseppe didn't seem to like people very much and hardly socialized. Most of the time, he stayed at home alone. Around this time, he started having an affair with the wife of a local bar owner, but it didn't last very long. She wanted him to spend too much money on her, which he didn't like to do.

On March 4, 1934, a series of murders began. A horticulturist, Marius Vassal, was sleeping under a tree after a long morning of work. He was shot to death, and his body was hidden under some light brush. His remains were found the following day. Police arrested a deranged man who always hung around the area. But two days after his arrest, the man was found dead in his cell, and the case was closed.

On August 5, 1934, an eighty-year-old man, Fernand Troin, was on his way home after buying food when, out of nowhere, a man shot and robbed him of his food and money. A postwoman who was working nearby heard the shot and saw the killer, a man, running from the scene. She would later describe the man to the police but, in court, could not identify Sasia.

On October 19, 1934, Sasia, who was friends with a thirty-five-year-old shepherd, Felicien Rouver, decided to break into Rouver's house and wait for him to return home that night. When Rouver entered his house, Sasia shot him to death and then stole his watch, handkerchief, and all the money he was carrying on him.

The following month, on November 30th, a twenty-six-year-old driver was murdered while he was working in the town of Verignon. The case was closed as a random robbery at first. But the police were now on guard and looking for a murderer around the area.

On December 7, 1934, Sasia was arrested by police officers patrolling the railway between Les Arcs and Vidauban. Sasia was carrying a rifle. When they asked him for his hunting license, he admitted he didn't have one. They took him in for hunting without a license.

The police searched him back at the station and found one of the stolen watches that had been reported missing from one of the murder victims earlier that year. When confronted about the watch, Sasia admitted to murdering the man who he stole the watch from.

Investigators searched Sasia's home later that day and found many items that had been stolen from the recently murdered men in the area, including watches and wallets. He was charged with four premeditated murders, theft, and highway robbery with aggravated circumstances.

Sasia was tried at the Assize Court on November 5, 1935, and even though he had admitted to two of the murders, he claimed that both were in self-defense. He claimed that he was innocent of the other two murders. Sasia was examined by a psychiatrist who judged him to be sane and fit to stand trial.

It only took less than an hour for the jury to convict Sasia of all four murders. He was sentenced to the death penalty. On the day he was convicted, over five hundred people were inside and outside the courtroom waiting to hear the sentence.

After Sasia was convicted, he appealed the verdict and sentence. He was rejected in both cases. He then asked to see a chaplain to beg for forgiveness. His lawyer was granted a visit with the president to get his case overturned, but that didn't work either.

Everyone had to wait for the guillotine to arrive at the city as there were only a few in use at that time, and other convicted murderers were waiting to be hanged. On February 17, 1936, at six in the morning, Sasia was executed by guillotine outside the prison walls. The public was restricted from seeing it.

This case caused controversy between Italy and France because Sasia was an Italian citizen. When he was first convicted, he was supposed to be deported, but he wasn't.

EIGHT

Casimir Dankerque

THE ARTOIS KILLER

Casimir Dankerque was born in Dainville, France, sometime in 1904. His birth date or location is unknown. What is known is that his father was a coal merchant. He had two siblings, and his parents never seemed to get along, fighting often in front of the children. Casimir was considered odd by most of his neighbors and classmates.

Casimir married in 1924, and the couple had three children together. He never had a regular steady job but worked as a laborer for short-term projects. Tired of Casimir's undependable behavior and never working or making enough money, his wife left him in 1930, taking the children with her.

Not long after she left, on April 23, 1930, Casimir was arrested for kidnapping a minor by a policeman who caught him in the act. While he was behind bars waiting to go on trial for the kidnapping, a police informant was put in the cell with him. He told the informant that he had broken into the local church two different times, having stolen valuables that were in a large trunk. He also admitted having stolen at least twenty-seven bikes in the last two months. The informant told the police what he admitted, and those crimes were added to his charges. He was sentenced to two years in prison.

When Casimir was released in 1933, he continued his life of crime. While his father was alive, he often accompanied him when delivering coal to different houses in the area. He remembered the wealthier customers and decided they would make his best targets.

Two older sisters owned the first house he robbed: one was seventy-three, and the other was ninety years old. They had lived alone for several years. On September 23, 1935, he entered their home from an unlocked back door and hid in a closet until it was late.

Figuring that the old ladies were in bed asleep, Casimir started going through their kitchen, looking for food. Out of nowhere, the ninety-year-old entered the kitchen. She began to scream when she saw him. Casimir reacted by kicking her to the ground, grabbing a large stick, and beating her. He couldn't leave her alive, so he grabbed a rope and strangled her to death. Once she was dead, he continued to go through the kitchen, taking things that he wanted and placing them into a bag.

Then, the seventy-three-year-old came into the kitchen. When she saw Casimir and then her sister lying on the floor, she began to scream. Casimir quickly pushed her onto the ground, jumped on top of her, and began to hit her until she passed out. He stole almost 2000 francs and some food, then ran. The following morning, a neighbor discovered the crime scene and called police. The seventy-three-year-old sister was taken to the hospital and survived her wounds.

Casimir spent the money he stole within the month, but after pulling off his first burglary, he figured he would have no problem doing it again. This time, he chose his neighbors to rob. They, too, were an older couple in their sixties.

On October 26th, he made his move. He went to their front door and knocked on it. Then, he hid in the front bushes by the door and waited for someone to answer. The wife opened the door and looked around until she saw someone standing in the bushes, making her jump and yell. He quickly jumped out of the bush and hit her with a stick. She fell to the ground while he was beating her, and the stick broke. She started to scream again. He bent down, quickly dragged her into their house, and closed the front door. He then began kicking he in the head until she stopped moving.

Casimir started rummaging through the house, grabbing anything he thought might be sold quickly and placing it into a bag. When he entered the bedroom, the man was sitting in a wheelchair and only partially dressed. He grabbed the man and shook him, then started punching him in the face and head and threw the man onto the floor. He wasn't moving either. He finished ransacking the house and left. This time, he managed to get about 2200 francs as well as some jewelry. Neighbors, hearing the noise, checked the house, found the bodies, and summoned the police.

The day after the couple was murdered, the police were notified by a pawnshop owner that a man had brought in some jewelry, rings, and over one thousand francs. Once police heard it was Casimir, they began searching for him. He was found sitting in a coffee shop. They arrested him and brought him in for questioning.

Once Casimir was asked where he got the large sum of money and jewelry, he had several vague answers. The police verified who owned the jewelry and confronted him again with this new information. He soon confessed to the robbery and murders of the couple. Detectives asked him to tell them all the details of his crime and got him to write and sign a statement about it.

The following morning, the police took him to the couple's house and asked him to reenact the crimes. While Casimir was describing the murders and why he decided to rob the couple, he let it slip that he had committed the same crime a month earlier and learned much from that robbery.

After more interrogations, Casimir admitted

that he had robbed both houses and murdered three people. He was charged with three murders, one attempted murder, and two robberies.

The trial went quickly, and on May 20, 1936, he was convicted on all counts and sentenced to death. Casimir was executed on August 13, 1936, by guillotine in front of a large crowd of people who were able to witness the whole event.

NINE

Eugen Weidmann

Eugen Weidmann was born in Frankfurt, Germany, on February 5, 1908. His father was a successful businessman—an exporter of goods—and his family lived an above-average lifestyle for the time. When World War I broke out, his father went to fight. Eugen was sent to live with his grandparents. While living there, he began stealing things any chance he could.

Eugen continued this penchant for thievery even after graduating from school. In his early twenties, he was caught and arrested. He was sentenced to five years in jail in Saarbrucken prison. While there, he became close to two men, Roger Million and Jean Blanc, who were also in prison for stealing.

After all three men were released in 1936, they decided to get a place to live together and started planning how to make some quick money. They rented an apartment in Paris and began looking for tourists visiting the country. They planned to rob them.

The first man they tried to kidnap and rob put up such a fight that they ended up letting him go and fleeing the scene. On the second attempt, they decided they would take more time to find out who they were about to rob.

Weidmann met Jean De Koven, a twenty-two-year-old dancer from New York, on July 27, 1937. He was visiting her aunt, who lived in Paris. They made plans to meet and go out the following night. Jean thought Weidmann was handsome and was excited about meeting him. Before she went to bed, she wrote a letter to her best friend who lived back in New York and told her about going to meet the man the next day.

The next day, Jean visited Weidmann, and the two of them went to his apartment, where she took photos of him with her new camera. After that, the pair went out to his garden to smoke. And that's when he strangled her to death.

Before he buried her body in that garden, he took her money and traveler's cheques from her purse. One of Weidmann's accomplices, Million, had his girlfriend, Colette Tricot, cash the murdered girls' traveler's cheques for them. Weidmann then sent a letter to the murdered girl's family telling them that they had kidnapped Jean and they would let her go if she gave them five hundred American dollars. Jean's brother traveled to Paris and offered 10,000 francs for any information about Jean's whereabouts.

Weidmann hired a driver, Joseph Couffy, to take him to the French Riviera on September 1st. Once they arrived, he shot Couffy in the back of the head when they stopped and were walking through a nearby forest. He then stole Couffy's car and about 2500 francs that the driver had made from other jobs. Weidmann returned home with the stolen car that they used to help them lure and murder more victims.

On September 3rd, they targeted a private nurse and told her they had a job for her. They arrived at her home, picked her up, and drove her to a forest. They forced her into a cave, where they shot her dead and stole over 1400 francs and a diamond ring from her body.

A month later, Weidmann arranged a meeting with a theater play producer, Roger LeBlond, telling him they were interested in investing in the man's shows. At their meeting, Weidmann shot the man in the back of his head and took his wallet, which had about 5000 francs in it.

On November 22nd, Weidmann arranged to meet a man he was once in prison with by inviting him to their apartment. For some reason, that man was murdered and buried in the same garden that Jean was buried in. It wasn't likely a robbery as the man wasn't working and lived poorly.

Five days later, Weidmann went to a realtor, Raymond Lesobre, and asked to see some properties in the Saint-Cloud district. While being shown a house, Weidmann shot the realtor in the back of his head and stole 5000 francs from him.

About one week later, after detectives found a business card belonging to Weidmann at the murdered realtor's office, they went to question him at his apartment. Weidmann wasn't home when they arrived, so they waited. When Weidmann returned home, he invited the three officers into his apartment and shut the door behind them. He then pulled his gun out and shot at them. The officers were wounded but were still able to wrestle Weidmann to the ground and knocked him out before arresting him and taking him back to the police station.

Once Weidmann regained consciousness, he was questioned by police. He confessed to all of the murders and robberies. Police arrested his two accomplices as well, and all three of them were charged with six counts of murder and several charges of theft. All three were found guilty.

Weidmann and Million were both sentenced to death, and Blanc received a twenty-month prison sentence. Tricot was acquitted of all charges. Milion's sentence was later reduced to life imprisonment.

Weidmann was executed by the guillotine on June 17, 1939, outside of the Saint-Pierre prison in Versailles, with anybody from the public allowed to watch. His execution was also filmed, and actor Christopher Lee was one of the members of the public who had watched the execution and was caught in the film.

TEN

Bernard Pesquet

THE LANDRU OF VAL-D'OISE

Bernad Pesquet was born in Heugleville-sur-Scie, France, on March 18, 1922. When Pesquet turned nine years old, his mother died, and he went to live with his grandfather. His grandfather's new wife did not like him, and the two fought constantly. At the age of fourteen, he was sent to a boarding school. Later that same year, Pesquet started working at a glass factory. He worked that job for about one year, and when he turned sixteen in 1938, he took a job working for his uncle as a cook in Rouen. About a month into this new job, he quit after arguing with his uncle at the restaurant.

The following year, Pesquet, unemployed, was caught stealing at a store and arrested. He was tried and acquitted of the charges as none of the witnesses of the theft showed up to testify. Meanwhile, he had been working to get his radio electrician ticket, and on March 18, 1939, his eighteenth birthday, he passed the exam. The new trade certificate allowed him to move away from the boarding house and into his apartment, which he used as both his living quarters and workshop.

In the following year, after the German occupation of France, he was required to work with a German soldier, Foyers, every morning. Foyers, or another German soldier, drove him around to the different areas he needed to work in throughout the day. During the workday, he never talked to anybody else and remained silent unless asked a direct question. Most people figured him to be weird.

Within the first year of his new job working for the Germans, in 1941, he met a young man, Julien Quibel, who was a few years older in his early twenties. The two became lovers. While they were together, Pesquet discovered that Quibel was an informer for the Germans. Nobody around them knew they were a couple. They just thought they were friends.

On the night of August 22, 1941, after the two of them went to bed, Pesquet attacked Quibel with an iron bar, beating him over the head. Once he lost consciousness, Pesquet slashed Quibel's veins and let him bleed out on the bed until he died.

Sometime in the middle of the night, Pesquet dragged Quibel's body out into a small patch of bush located a couple of blocks from where he lived. The following day, when the body was discovered, police questioned people who lived around that area. They soon learned from one of Pesquet's neighbors that Quibel had been staying overnight with Pesquet for a few weeks. Investigators suspected that the two men might have been sexually involved with each other.

Three days later, on August 25, 1941, police came to Pesquet's apartment and arrested him. It took three days before he admitted to killing

Quibel. Pesquet claimed that he murdered him for two reasons: firstly, Quibel was informing the Germans about the French people and was a traitor, and secondly, and most likely the main reason, was to steal his savings from him.

Pesquet was formally charged with murder, and because he was between the ages of sixteen and nineteen, he was facing the death penalty. But at his young age, it was unlikely.

On November 8, 1941, the court found Pesquet guilty of murder and sentenced him to life imprisonment with hard labor and no chance of parole. As suspected, he was spared the death sentence. The prison was overwhelmed with inmates at the time Pesquet entered. The surplus of prisoners was mainly due to the war, but it was also because suspected resistance members were placed there by the Germans. The excess number of inmates led to a shortage of food for the prisoners. Some of them even starved to death while in captivity.

On May 8, 1945, the prisoner conditions became better as the war ended and France was liberated from Germany. Pesquet was now twenty-three years old and decided to request a new trial, but it was rejected in July of the same year.

In 1951, the country lightened its prison

sentences and started to allow prisoners who had committed murders and other heinous crimes to apply for parole. Later, in 1960, the government abolished the hard labor prisons in France. These changes automatically allowed prisoners like Pesquet to apply for parole. With the time he had served, he was allowed to use it anytime after August 1956, which had already passed.

Pesquet successfully made parole on October 12, 1961, because he had a clean record for the whole time he had been in prison, not breaking the rules once in twenty years. Now, at thirty-nine years old, he returned home and started to work as a painter.

Within a few years, he met and married twenty-year-old Christine Ruax in 1968. The couple moved to Pierrelaye in the early part of 1973. Sometime in 1974, Pequet's wife learned about his history of murder, serving twenty years in prison. She also discovered that he was a homosexual, which caused her to want a divorce.

The revelation of his past also caused significant tension between the couple, who now fought almost daily. During one of those battles, Pesquet got his rifle and shot his wife in the head. Surprisingly, the wound didn't immediately kill her. But it did make her suffer. He just left her on the bed until she finally died a few hours later. He buried her body in the ground of the basement of their house.

After about a week, some neighbors came over and asked to see Christine. Pesquet told them that she had decided to leave him. He also wrote a letter to her parents telling them that she left him and that he was sorry for that. Everyone believed these stories, including her family. They knew the couple had been fighting, and she was depressed. Christine had previously taken out a small loan from a bank, and they were looking for her to pay it back, but after a few months, they decided to write the amount owed off.

Henri Franqui, a fifty-two-year-old realtor, came to Pesquet's home to ask him if he was interested in selling the house now that he was alone. Pesquet was bothered by Franqui, so he let him in the house and shot him with his rifle. He then buried his body in the basement right beside his wife's body. He then sold the realtor's car and used his checkbook to buy various things he needed.

Pesquet was still trying to work as a painter and regularly placed ads in the newspaper. An older couple in Neuilly-sur-Seine had answered one of his ads, asking him to come out and meet them to discuss what needed to be done and how much it would be. He replied to the couple that he would arrive at their house on July 29, 1975, around noon.

Pesquet arrived about 11:30 that morning, where the owners of the house, seventy-one-year-old Emile Bergaud and his wife, seventy-three-year-old Alice, along with their servant, sixty-three-year-old Alfeia Borgioni, were all getting ready to have lunch. Pesquet entered the home and, after talking with them for a short while, luring them into trusting him, went out to his car, got his rifle, returned to the house, and shot and killed all three of them. After taking all the money and valuables that he could find, he got in his car and returned home.

The bodies were discovered the next day, and while the investigators were searching the crime scene, they found the letter that came from Pesquet saying that he would be arriving on the same day that the murders happened.

Detectives checked into Pesquet's background and learned about his twenty years in prison for a previous murder, so they went to his place. They arrested him and brought him in for questioning. After searching his house, police also found some of the jewelry and personal possessions belonging to other victims. Even after he was presented with all the evidence, he remained completely silent.

The police, becoming even more suspicious of Pesquet, searched his home again. During the second search, on August 11, 1976, they found the two bodies, Christine Pesquet and Henri Franqui, buried in his basement. When the investigators confronted him about finding the bodies, Pesquet confessed to those two murders immediately. The press called him the Landru du Val-d'Oise as he had murdered both his wife and a realtor, just as serial killer Henri Landru did in the past. (Chapter 5)

Finally, on June 18, 1982, Pesquet was tried for the murders of his wife, Christine Pesquet, the realtor, Henri Franqui, and the three residences of the house he was supposed to paint in Neuilly-sur-Seine in July 1982. This trial would be a very lengthy one, taking over six years to complete.

Pesquet had a defense of a crime of passion in his wife's murder. He claimed that he murdered the realtor only because the realtor had constantly harassed him and continuously came to his home, trying to get him to sell it, which made him angry. He gave no defense for the triple murders of the homeowners, saying he had nothing to do with it.

He was convicted of all six murders and

sentenced to life imprisonment. Pesquet would successfully appeal his conviction, and they would have to retry him again.

He was found guilty at that time as well and sentenced to life in prison again. Pesquet died while in prison on May 10, 2009, when he was eighty-seven years old.

ELEVEN

Albert Millet

THE WILD BOARD OF THE MOORS

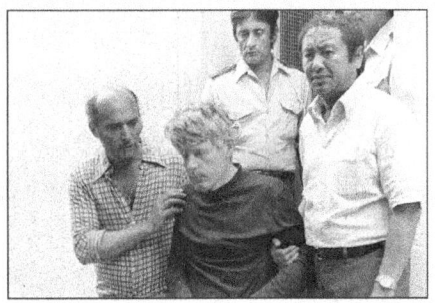

Albert Pierre Millet was born in Hyeres, France, on July 2, 1929. His mother didn't like having children and never took care of her son whenever she happened to be at home. She had a lover with whom she would spend most of her time. His father was an angry alcoholic who often beat him.

By the age of fourteen, Millet dropped out of

school and usually hung around the streets looking for an opportunity to steal something. When he committed a robbery or theft, he often hid in a maquis area—a large area of densely grown shrubs—on the outskirts of town.

In 1950, when he reached the age of twenty-one, Millet had to serve his mandatory two years of military service. He was trained to be a sniper. While in the army, he continued his behavior of stealing, usually from other soldiers. Eventually, he was caught in the act, and he got into a fight with the officer. This conduct led to him being tried and convicted by the military for theft and assault of an officer. In June 1961, he tried to kill an Algerian teenager by shooting him but was caught in the act and stopped. Again, he was tried and convicted of the crime, but this time, he was sent to a military prison.

Millet was released from military prison and discharged in early 1954. He returned home, where he met and fell in love with Paulette Dogliotti, a fifteen-year-old student who lived with her aunt. Shortly after they started seeing each other, Dogliotti's aunt forbade them from seeing each other anymore, as her niece was far too young to be involved that seriously with anybody.

Millet agreed to stop seeing Dogliotti without

a fight. But about a month later, in March 1954, Millet entered the bar where Dogliotti's aunt was out with her fiancé and began yelling at her and calling her names for not letting him see her niece. The aunt's fiancé slapped him across his face and threw him out of the bar. A while later, Millet came back in and calmly walked over to the couple and told them that he was going to kill them both, then left the bar.

On March 28th, around dinner time, Dogliotti's aunt walked her to a bus stop as she was going to visit some other family. They were both sitting at the bus stop when Millet came out of nowhere, walked up to them, shot at Paulette, his ex-girlfriend, and ran. A few days later, on April 3rd, he went to Dogliotti's aunt's house to apologize to them both. When the aunt saw him, she began to scream at him. He pulled out his gun and shot her dead.

After the murder, Millet went and hid in the maquis as he usually did after he robbed someone. The following day, he tried to leave town by train. The police were on the lookout for him, believing that he might try to flee the city. They saw him at the train station, and during his apprehension, they shot him three times, but he survived his wounds, even though he went into a coma.

When he finally recovered, he was charged with one count of murder and one count of attempted murder and faced trial on September 30, 1955. During court, Millet told the jury that he had no intention of killing Dogliotti. He claimed that if he had wanted to kill her, he wouldn't have missed.

In response to murdering the girl's aunt, he claimed that when he went to the house, the aunt had agreed to go with him to the police station and withdraw the charges she made against him for attempting to shoot her niece. Still, while they were leaving, she went crazy and started yelling for no reason. He said he panicked and shot her.

The jury didn't believe him, and he was convicted of both charges. While waiting to be sentenced, he filed an appeal of the conviction, which was overturned because of a technicality. He was retried again in March 1956. Again, he was convicted but, this time, sentenced to life imprisonment.

During his imprisonment, he was considered a model prisoner who made significant contributions to the guards, and therefore, his sentence was reduced to only twenty years.

While in prison, Millet started writing to the wife of one of his friends, Fernande Valentin, a nurse's aide in the hospital at San Salvador in Hyeres. Soon after, she divorced her husband and began visiting Millet in prison. Over the following few visits, the couple decided to get married once he was released from jail.

On July 10, 1973, Millet, now forty-four years old, was released from prison on parole. Within a month, the two got married and moved into a house in Hyeres. Valentin paid for their expenses because Millet could not find a regular job. He claimed it was because of his criminal record.

Over the next few years, Millet became possessive of Valentin and wanted to know where she was every minute of the day. He started to think that she was having an affair with someone else at her work. They began to quarrel over this more and more often. After working all day, she would return home and try to go to sleep, and he would demand sex from her. If she didn't have sex with him, he would say that was because she had another boyfriend who she was having sex with.

By the Summer of 1979, Valentin was tired of constantly working just to come home and be accused of cheating. She told him that she was going to leave him and get a divorce and that she no longer wanted to work every day to pay all the expenses when he did nothing. She also told him that she would give him 20,000 francs so he could afford to live on his own for a while until he got resettled.

On the morning of June 13, 1979, Millet stabbed Valentin several times in her face, head, and chest while she was still in bed sleeping. She died from her wounds almost immediately. He went into the kitchen and began to drink alcohol. As he got drunk, he decided to get ready for the police, who he knew would be soon coming. He barricaded himself in the house.

The screaming and noise from when Millet was attacking Valentin earlier caused the neighbors to call the police. They said that they feared something terrible might be happening next door. Two officers responded to the call. When they arrived, they walked up to the front door and knocked. Millet began shooting at them from one of the windows. The officers returned to the car and called for backup. It wasn't long before more police surrounded the house. It took a couple of hours before they convinced Millet to surrender.

During Millet's first interview with the police, he claimed that after he murdered Valentin, he had planned to take his own life as well as their pet dog. He took their dog to the maquis but couldn't go through with it. He said he set the dog free and came home alone. Later, the police found the couple's dog dead, having been hung by a rope in a field.

Millet was charged with his wife's murder, and his trial began on May 11, 1981. When the jury found him guilty of murder, they decided that it was not premeditated but, instead, murder in the second degree. He was still sentenced to life in prison.

Millet was a model prisoner, just as he was the first time he was in jail. And once again, his sentence was reduced to twenty-five years. In 1999 and 2000, Millet was granted day passes where he used to go to the city of Nice and stay in a hotel.

On his fourth day out on furlough, he met fifty-year-old Gisele at a coffee shop. The two chatted for a while, and he told her about his past criminal activities. She didn't seem bothered by them. Gisele lived alone on her pension and spent most of her time gambling it away at a casino. The two ended up becoming involved until he returned to prison.

On December 20, 2001, Millet was released from prison on parole. He moved in with Gisele in Nice. The couple got along well until the following year when Millet became possessive and controlling over her. Gisele decided she wanted him to leave her apartment and break up. Millet told her that he had stolen twelve gold bars, hid them in the maquis and that she could have them if she stayed with him. The two took a cab to the deserted location to get the gold. Once the cab driver left, she became worried and fled the area. She made it out to the main road and was able to hitchhike back to Nice.

The following day, Millet showed up at her apartment, and she let him in. He stayed four nights, and then she told him she wanted him to leave again the following day. In the morning, he attacked her with a kitchen knife. He fled the apartment, and she called for an ambulance.

Millet went to his parole officer and confessed what he had done. He was arrested and charged with attempted murder. He was tried the following year, convicted, and sentenced to seven years. He ended up serving five and a half of the seven years and was rereleased on parole in August 2007. He was seventy-eight years old by now.

Millet returned to Hyeres and moved into a hotel where he could live off his savings, about 30,000 euros while working in prison. Millet met one of his neighbors, a younger woman named Chantal, who was unemployed and struggling financially. He offered to have her move in with him and told her he would support her.

Soon after Chantel moved in with Millet, he became angry because she started having a friend over every day. Christian Fernandez, a forty-one-year-old man she had known for a couple of years. They had a big argument in which Millet demanded that Chantel pay him back everything he had ever spent on her.

Things were calm around the apartment for the next month until November 17, 2007, when Chantel invited Christian back. Millet ignored them and went to bed. Christian and Chantel stayed up drinking and talking, but they were making too much noise for Millet, who had to come out of his room and tell them to be quiet a few times.

Early the following day, when Millet got up, he found Christian was still there. He went back into his room and got his gun. When he came out, Chantel was on the sofa beside Christian. Millet got angry and shot her in the leg. Then he turned the gun towards Christian and shot him three times, killing him.

Millet left the hotel and went to the maquis to hide. There, he would shoot himself in the head.

TWELVE

Andre Robini

THE OLD LADY KILLER

Andre Robini was born in Nice, France, on April 29, 1928. He lived with his unhappy parents, who didn't get along well. He attended school until he graduated from grade eight and began working as a baker after that. His mother died suddenly, leaving him in a state of shock. He quit his job and did nothing.

He now lived alone with his father, whom he constantly fought. At night, he would go out and walk around the town streets with no intention but to get away from his father. But one night, he got into some minor trouble when a shop owner accused him of stealing something, and they got into a scuffle. The police arrested Robini, and he was placed in a juvenile detention school. While in detention, his father committed suicide by shooting himself in the head.

When he was released in the Summer of 1945, he volunteered in the French Union Army, an army whose purpose was to fight far-east battles for France in the Pacific. He trained in the paratrooper division and was promoted to sergeant over time. Robini was then sent to fight in the First Indochina War. That ended in July 1954, and the army was demobilized.

In the Spring of 1955, Robini began a spree of murders. He would walk the streets, looking for older ladies who were alone, perhaps out shopping or running errands. He would then follow them until they were in a relatively isolated location, assault them, and then flee.

In May, he dared to further his advances by, instead of assaulting them on the street, he chose to follow them to their home. Once he knew that they were alone, he would break into their home, tie them up, and beat them into unconsciousness. He then looted their house, taking any valuables and money that he could find.

Robini's first known victim was on May 28, 1955, when he followed seventy-seven-year-old Antoinette Broquerie to her home on Rue de Levis. After he got into her place, he grabbed her, gagged her mouth, and tied her to a chair. He pulled out his knife, sliced open her throat, and ransacked her home, leaving with her valuables while she was left to bleed to death.

On January 20, 1956, Robini followed a seventy-seven-year-old retired newspaper saleswoman, Marie Chenaud, to her home on Rue des Martyrs. He waited until she went to bed before breaking into her place. While still sleeping in her bed, he attacked and beat her. Chenaud's head was hit so hard that it had been dislocated from the occipital bone. Even with such an injury, it wasn't the cause of her death. She was then suffocated to death by a small towel that had been shoved deeply down her throat.

Robini's next attack was less than a week later when Robini followed Marguerite Meurdac, a seventy-two-year-old retired journalist, to her apartment in Boulogne-Billancourt. When her body was discovered the following day, she had been viciously attacked with a knife and stabbed over twenty times.

Robini's next assault would be his final one on February 28, 1956. He followed another older woman, just as he had done before, but for some reason, he decided to attack her before she got into her apartment building. While he was trying to subdue her, she was able to resist him enough not only to scream but to throw him off his balance, and he fell. The noise from the scuffle attracted several people who witnessed the assault. One of the witnesses was a postal worker who carried a gun with him, and he pulled it out and threatened Robini with it. Robini fled the scene and ran into an office building next door. Two police officers followed him into the building and called for backup. Soon, the whole building was surrounded, and eventually, Robini surrendered without any significant fight.

From the time when Robini was dismissed from the army in 1955 until he was eventually caught in February 1956, there were not only the three murders of elderly ladies detailed above, but at least forty other attacks committed the same way. The victims were either stabbed, strangled, and sometimes even shot, but they all survived their wounds.

Robini ended up being charged with three murders and thirteen assaults. The court ordered a mental evaluation on him to ensure he was competent enough to stand trial. He was diagnosed as a perverted gerontophobe without any regard for other people's well-being. This diagnosis still allowed him to know the difference between right and wrong, and he was permitted to go to trial.

The trial was quick and only lasted two days. Robini was found guilty of all charges and given the death sentence. His sentence was later commuted to life imprisonment after the death penalty was abolished in France. On August 7, 1978, Robini was pardoned by the president of France for no given reason. He was released after only serving about eighteen years in prison. He later died on June 28, 2001.

THIRTEEN

Tommy Recco

GERONIMO

J oseph-Thomas "Tommy" Recco was born in Propriano, Corsica, France, on May 10, 1934. It is assumed he is nicknamed Geronimo because of his long hair and resemblance to the Native American Apache military leader Geronimo.

In the early Summer of 1960, Tommy and his younger brother Pierre were fishing using dynamite. The two boys were seen by Tommy's godfather, Casabianca, who happened to be a marine guard. Afraid they would be caught for poaching, Tommy told Pierre to wait in the boat. Tommy went and got his rifle and shot his godfather. He then walked up to the body and beat his godfather's head several times with the butt of the rifle. To make sure that he was dead, he picked up a large stone and dropped it on Casabianca's head. He returned to the boat where his younger brother had been waiting for him, and the two went fishing again. Pierre noticed the blood on Tommy's hand and asked him what happened, but Tommy just changed the subject and never told him what he did.

Later that same day, a couple walking the beach discovered Casabianca's body and called for the police. When police arrived, they spotted wood chips around the body, which they determined had probably come from the butt of a rifle. Their first thought was that Casabianca had seen some poachers, and they killed him.

For some unknown reason, rumors began to spread that Tommy Recco was the person who murdered Casabianca. It was unclear whether people in town didn't like Tommy or his brother Pierre and had started saying that Tommy had something to do with what had happened that day. Upon hearing the stories going around town, the police questioned Tommy.

Tommy told police that he knew nothing about what happened to his godfather and he would never have hurt him for any reason. Tommy's mother supported him, telling the police her son could never do such a thing. His mother was already grieving at the time because one of her other brothers had been killed, along with his son, in a car accident.

A couple of months later, Pierre, during an interview with the police, told them about the two of them out fishing with dynamite that day. He also said that when they went back to the shore, and while he waited in the boat for Tommy, he heard gunshots and his godfather screaming before Tommy returned to the boat.

Investigators brought Tommy back in for more questioning. He continued to deny any responsibility for the murder until they confronted him with his brother, Pierre's, signed statement. Tommy broke down and confessed that he had murdered his godfather as he didn't want to be arrested and have to pay a fine for using dynamite to catch fish. He told police that, for some reason, he had just snapped and couldn't control himself.

Tommy was formally charged, and his trial

began on December 8, 1962. At the trial, Tommy retracted his confession but was still found guilty of murder and sentenced to death. He appealed his sentence of death, and it was denied. Later, his sentence was pardoned by Charles de Gaulle, and he was commuted to a term of life in prison.

While Tommy was in prison, his family had gone through a lot of trauma and loss. Both of his brothers were murdered. Toussaint, his older brother, was killed by his brother-in-law during a fight in 1973, and Pierre was killed during a robbery by two hooded men in 1976. After that, his sister Francine fell down a flight of stairs and died from her injuries.

Tommy was a model prisoner while serving his fifteen-year prison term. He was released on parole in the Summer of 1977 and moved to Marseille to start over. He didn't want to live where he grew up, with so much loss having happened there. In Marseille, he worked in a diving shop selling diving suits and equipment.

A few years later, in December 1979, a supermarket located in the town of Beziers was robbed, and during that robbery, three cashiers were all shot to death by one gunshot to the back of the head execution style. A total sum of about 700,000 francs was stolen from the store. Police had difficulty finding any leads as no witnesses or evidence were left at the scene, so the case went cold.

In January 1980, an eleven-year-old girl from Carqueiranne was at home playing with her father when a man came by to talk to her father. He told her to go downstairs until he was done. About an hour later, the girl heard the two men yelling. She got scared, so she picked up the phone and called her mother, who was working at a children's school. Her mother had already left for home, so her supervisor took the call. During the call, the girl said her father argued with "Rene's cousin." The supervisor told her everything would be fine and that her mother would be home soon. The supervisor phoned Mr. and Mrs. Coutrix, the next-door neighbors to the little girl's family and friends to her and the girl's mother. After the call, Mr. Coutrix went to the girl's house to check on things. After about a half hour of him not returning home, Mrs. Coutrix decided she would also go over.

When Mrs. Coutrix arrived at the house, she knocked on the door and got no answer. She listened carefully but didn't hear a noise, so she tried to open the door. It was open. When she walked in, she found both her husband's and the little girl's bodies lying on the floor. She called the police immediately. After the police arrived, they searched the house and found the girl's father dead in the basement. Mrs. Coutrix told the detectives about the girl phoning the school and saying that her father was fighting with "Rene's cousin." When the mother returned home, she explained to them that "Rene's cousin" was Tommy Recco.

Police located where Recco lived and went to his place to take him in for questioning. During the interview, Recco denied knowing anything about the crime and claimed he hadn't been there that day. The police had to let him go as they had nothing to hold him on.

The next day, another detective went over and picked up Recco and took him to where the bodies were for identification. When Recco saw the little girl's body, he asked why it happened. The detective looked at him and replied, because of what you did. Recco then began to break down and started to explain what happened.

Recco claimed that he was at the house to buy a gun from the father, but they couldn't reach a deal and soon began to argue about the price. He admitted that he went into a rage and couldn't control himself, grabbed the gun, and killed the girl's father. He added that when he went upstairs and started to leave out the back door, he saw the neighbor, Mr. Coutrix, walking up to and entering the front door. He said that he panicked and went back into the house, where he shot Coutrix in the head. Then he noticed the little girl was standing there and saw everything, so he killed her as well before leaving.

Recco was charged with the three murders and placed in custody to await trial. Several newspapers began to report on Recco's arrest.

When the Bezier police, the town where the supermarket was held up, and the murders of three cashiers recently happened, heard about the triple murder case in Carqueiranne, they contacted the detectives who were in charge of the crime to see if there were any similarities between the two crimes. The obvious thing they noticed was that in both crimes, the victims were all shot to death. Comparing the ballistics report in both cases, they learned that the same weapon or type had been used. The Carqueiranne police interviewed Recco, but he denied everything.

In May 1980, a man walked into the police station in Bezier and asked to talk to the detectives in charge of the murder investigation that was in the newspapers. The man told the investigator that he recognized the man who had been arrested for the murders. He said he saw that same man in the grocery store in Bezier on the day that it was robbed and the cashiers were murdered.

Again, police questioned Recco about being in the grocery store that day, but he denied it. Another connection between Recco and the grocery store came up when they learned that Recco had delivered one of the diving suits he had sold to the grocery store only a week before it was robbed.

While Recco was in jail awaiting trial, in the Fall of 1981, two French tourists, both twenty-one-year-old women, disappeared from the area. Police learned about some rumors that Antoine Recco, Tommy's father, was involved in the crime as the girls were last seen with him. Police questioned Antonie about the girls, but he told them he couldn't remember them.

Upon searching his property, they found the swimsuits belonging to the missing women in one of Antonie's boats. Detectives detained Antoine and took him in for questioning. Soon, he confessed to having met the girls. They asked him to take them out for a boat ride, which he did. While they were out in the boat, he made sexual advances on them, but they both refused and laughed at him. Antonie strangled both of them to death in his boat, tied their bodies down with weights, and threw them into the water.

Antonie was charged with both murders, and in August 1986, he was convicted and sentenced to life imprisonment. Due to his medical issues, they released Antonie from prison in May 2010, and he moved to Corsica, where he still lives today.

On June 6, 1983, his son, Tommy Recco's, trial began. Throughout the trial, Tommy continued to claim that he was innocent. The court had ordered a psychiatric exam be done on Recco, and it was determined that he was fit to stand trial. Recco was found guilty of six murders and sentenced to life imprisonment. He has applied several times for medical release from prison, but all of his applications have been denied.

FOURTEEN

Marcel Barbeault

THE SHADOW KILLER

Marcel Henri Barbeault was born in Liancourt, France, on August 10, 1941. He is responsible for the murder of seven women and one man. Because his crimes were always in the evening or early morning, he was nicknamed "The Shadow Killer."

Barbeault's father worked as a steam train conductor, and his mother made clothes in a factory. He quit school at the age of thirteen, and by the time he turned fourteen, he began a full-time job working as a riveter in a machine shop. He also joined the Young Christian Workers, an international youth organization for young trade workers.

On December 13, 1960, after he turned nineteen, he joined the French Army and was sent to the Algerian War to work as a stretcher bearer. The war ended in 1962, and he returned home to his prior job as a riveter in the machine shop.

Barbeault decided to take up boxing and judo to become a policeman or a paratrooper in the army. He applied for both jobs at least eight times but was denied because he suffered from vertigo.

Barbeault married a woman, Josiane, in 1964, and the couple had two children: Patrice in 1964 and Laurent in 1972. Shortly after they had their first child, his mother died of cancer in 1968, and before their second child, both of his brothers also died.

After the deaths of his family members, Barbeault became violent. It was even argued that the deaths in his family were the catalyst for his violent tendencies. He began to burgle homes and steal weapons late at night after he got off of work. He also began to collect different weapons, such as knives and guns. It wasn't long before his crimes included murder.

Barbeault would start going to the railway tracks at night, usually between nine and eleven, looking for victims. He would strike them with a shovel to knock them over or unconscious. Then he would jump on top of them and stab them, always aiming for the heart. A few of his victims he would shoot with his rifle. He always chose women as victims, and women of color specifically. He would often have watched them for a while before attacking them. Once they were dead, he would remove all of their clothing, but he never had sex with any of them. When he returned home, he was calm, mild-mannered, and was never mean to his wife or children.

His first murder was on January 10, 1969, when he killed Françoise Lecron, wife of a Saint-Gobain engineer. These attacks and murders continued until January 1976, when police received an anonymous phone call saying that The Shadow Killer was Barbeault.

Detectives went to his house, detained him, and took him in for questioning. They searched his home and found the rifle that had killed some of the victims in his basement. They were able to gather enough evidence to charge him with five of the murders. However, there was not enough evidence to charge him officially with the other three murders attributed to him.

Barbeault's trial began on May 25, 1981, and on June 10, 1981, he was found guilty and sentenced to life imprisonment. He appealed his conviction, which was accepted, and his conviction was overturned. But on another appeal by the prosecutor, it was reinstated again. He remains in prison for life.

FIFTEEN

Michel Peiry

THE SADIST OF ROMONT

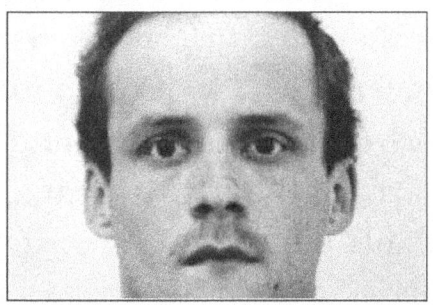

Michel Peiry was born in Romont, Switzerland, on February 28, 1959. Peiry is said to have had a difficult time as a child because his father was a bad alcoholic who would often punish him with lots of yelling and beatings. When Peiry turned fourteen, he tried to hide his homosexuality from his father. He went to one of the leaders of the Catholic Church to which his family belonged, and the man raped him.

After a member of the church raped him, he came across some photos of bondage. The images excited him. Soon after that, his sexual desires and the violence in his life from his father and the rape intermixed. The mixture was so intense that he was forever unable to have one without the other.

When Peiry turned sixteen, his family moved to Romont, and soon after they moved, he got a job as a waiter in a coffee shop. His customers were often part of the fringe communities, which included gay men and neo-nazis. He must have had some conversations with these men as later, a copy of Hitler's *Mein Kempf* was found in his room. The police arrested him for that, and he was forced to quit his job at the coffee shop and get a job in a factory.

By the early part of the 1980s, Peiry would begin a killing spree where he would go out driving and look for hitchhikers, usually younger men who were traveling alone. He would sexually assault the men, murder them, and burn their bodies.

Peiry's first known attack and murder happened on September 1, 1981, when Peiry was twenty-one. He had traveled to America for a visit and, while there, met a young Canadian man, Sylvestre, who was also touring around America. Soon after they met, Sylvestre vanished. Peiry later confessed to having murdered Sylvestre after he raped him with a hammer somewhere near Miami. Peiry later retracted his confession.

The next attack and murder Peiry was known to have committed was in February 1984 when he was in France. He was driving when he saw Frederic hitchhiking in the Annecy part of France. He sexually assaulted the man before murdering and burning his body.

In June 1985, Peiry murdered his only female victim, Anne-Laure. He met her in Sainted-Maries-de-la-Mer, Camargue. Not much is known about the victim or what exactly he did to her.

The following year, sometime in early May 1986, Peiry was back in Switzerland. He picked up a young man named Cedric, who was only fourteen. He sexually assaulted and murdered the boy, burned his body, and left it in Albinen, which is a very isolated part of Valais. His body was discovered on May 7, 1986.

During the Summer of that same year, Peiry started traveling regularly to many of the nearby European countries, where he continued his murder spree. He later confessed to the murder of a young man, Silvio, who he picked up and murdered in the Rijeka area of Croatia sometime in July. After that, he picked up Fabio on the night of August 15th. He repeated his pattern of rape, murder, and burning the body before leaving the country.

Sometime in early November, Peiry picked up sixteen-year-old Yves Ath and, after driving him into a secluded area, attacked him as well. The young man survived being sexually assaulted, beaten, and covered with gas. Peiry couldn't light Yves on fire because his matches were soaking wet from being outside in the rain, so he just drove off and left him there.

In March 1987, police discovered a dead young man, Vincent, sixteen years old, who had been sexually assaulted, murdered, and set on fire. Even though he was attacked and killed in the same manner as Peiry's previous victims, it was never definitively proven to be one of his victims.

The following month, on April 16, 1987, Peiry attacked a young man in France. He raped, murdered, and burned him also. This victim was only uncovered after one of Peiry's confessions.

On April 24th, he attacked his final victim, Thomas, who survived the attack. Around midnight, Peiry picked up the seventeen-year-old, who was hitchhiking home from the Place du Tunnel in Lausanne. Instead of taking the boy home, Peiry took him to a side road where nobody lived and stopped the car. He attacked Thomas, handcuffed him, and sexually assaulted him. After he had finished his attack, he hit Thomas on the head, knocking him out, and then threw his body into the river. But Thomas was not dead. He was able to get to shore and walked a few miles to get help. Thomas was able to give police a good description of his attacker and the make of his vehicle.

Police made a sketch composite of the attacker and the vehicle he was driving, which was placed in newspapers and cities. It wasn't long before Peiry was arrested on May 1, 1987. He confessed to several of the attacks and murders.

After a medical exam ordered by the court, Peiry was found sane, and his trial proceeded. On October 31, 1989, Peiry was found guilty of sexually assaulting four minors. With the lack of proof of the other offenses that Peiry committed, he was not found guilty. He was sentenced to life imprisonment and allowed to apply for parole after serving fifteen years.

SIXTEEN

Roberto Succo

THE FULL MOON ASSASSIN

R oberto Succo was born in Mestre, Venice, Italy, on April 3, 1962. His father, Nazario, was fifty-three years old and worked for Commissioner La Barbera. His mother, Maria, was forty years old and a stay-at-home mother.

Succo was an average student in school. However, he never got along with many classmates and didn't make friends easily. He was short-tempered and often yelled at people for little things. He loved science class and enjoyed dissecting small animals or fish.

During the Easter weekend in 1981, at nineteen, Roberto wanted to use his father's car, but his mother didn't want him to. She was always scared he would wreck the car and get into an accident. When his father let him have the car a few times before, she would go to bed until he returned home. On the holiday weekend, Roberto asked to use the car on Saturday but was turned down. He asked again on Sunday, but his mother scolded him this time and again wouldn't let him take the car.

After the second refusal, he walked into the kitchen, grabbed a knife, went to his mother's room, and stabbed her thirty-two times in the head and neck until she died. He then dragged her body and put it into the bathtub. Roberto turned off all the lights in the house and waited in his bedroom until his father came home from work.

Nazario got home a little after eleven that night, and after he walked into the house, Roberto attacked him from behind using an axe. His father put up a fight. Even after being hit a few times with the axe, he managed to wrestle it away from Roberto. The fight continued until Roberto was able to reach a nylon bag, wrap it around his father's face, and suffocate him. He then put his father's body on top of his mother's in the tub, covered their bodies with lime, and filled the tub with water. Roberto grabbed his father's car keys and gun and left. He fled from Mestre.

After police discovered the bodies of both of Roberto's parents, they started to search for him. Two days later, they found him in a pizzeria eating in San Pietro al Natisone, which was close to the Yugoslovakia border, and arrested him.

The court gave Roberto a psychiatric exam and found him to have a mental illness. They placed him in a psychiatric prison for ten years in Reggio Emilia. While in the hospital, he started to study geology through correspondence from the University of Parman. He was a well-behaved patient who never got into trouble.

After five years in the hospital, and because he was such a good patient and doctors thought he was recovering well, Roberto was allowed to go out in the day for short periods. On May 15, 1986, he left and never came back to the hospital.

He evaded the police by taking the train to France using a fake name.

For the next three years, Roberto would commit several crimes not only in France but in Switzerland and Italy as well. He burglarized homes, raped women, and even murdered again. In France, he ended up murdering two police officers, a doctor, and two women after raping them.

On February 28, 1988, Roberto returned to his hometown in Mestre and was spotted by someone who once knew him. They reported the sighting to the police, and he was later arrested.

On May 23, 1988, he committed suicide in his cell by suffocating himself with a plastic bag.

SEVENTEEN

Thierry Paulin

THE GRIM REAPER OF PARIS

Thierry Paulin was born in Fort-de-France, Martinique, on November 28, 1963. Just after his birth, his father, a French airline pilot, left him and his mother, who was still a teenager herself. Paulin was then sent to live with his grandmother, who lived in Martinique. However, because she ran a busy restaurant, she left him alone most of the time.

Just after Paulin turned ten, his mother got remarried and sent for him to come live with her and her new husband. His mother's new husband also had children from his first marriage, with whom Paulin didn't get along very well. After being in several fights and acting out too much for them, Paulin's mother asked his biological father to take him to mainland France. He agreed in exchange for not having to pay her alimony anymore.

Paulin finished school at seventeen and joined the military, serving in the logistics branch of the Air Force of France. He wasn't well-liked by the other soldiers he served with. According to him, they didn't like him because he was of mixed race and because he was gay.

Paulin's first known crime was on November 12, 1982, when he was shopping in a grocery store. He pulled a knife out of his jacket and robbed an older lady who was also shopping there. After he got her money, he fled the scene quickly, but the store clerk recognized him and told the police. He was arrested the following June 1983 and charged with the robbery. He was convicted and sent to prison for a two-year suspended sentence, which allowed him to be accessible only if he got into trouble, and he would have to serve two years in jail. He was also discharged from the army because of his criminal conviction.

In 1984, Paulin returned to living with his mother and her new family, who were now living in the suburbs of Paris. Their relationship didn't improve, and he would often get into fights with every family member. During this time, he got a job working as a waiter in a gay club, which frequently had drag show performances. While working his new job, he watched several shows and eventually started to dress in drag and perform himself. Paulin soon felt confident enough to invite his mother to watch one of the shows, but she left a few seconds after he came out on stage.

While Paulin was working at the club, he (she) met Jean-Thierry, a nineteen-year-old, and the two started dating. Thierry was a drug addict, and eventually, Paulin began using illegal drugs regularly as well.

To make extra money to pay for the illicit drugs they were using, Paulin started to sell them at the club. Around this time, in October 1984, older women began getting robbed, and some of them were murdered in their homes.

On October 5th, ninety-one-year-old Germaine Petitot and eighty-three-year-old Anna Barbier-Ponthus were attacked, beaten, and robbed in their home. After the thief got their money, he attempted to suffocate them by using the pillows from their bed. Barbier-Ponthus died from the attack, but Petitot lived but was unable to give very many details of the attack to the police.

Over the next two months, at least eight more women were murdered during these types of attacks. They were all murdered in very aggressive ways, such as being forced to drink Draino, being suffocated by a plastic bag held over their head, or being roughly beaten. In all cases, the motive was robbery.

The neighborhood became a terror, and the police presence became intense. Paulin and Mathurin decide to go to Toulouse and stay with Paulin's father for a few months until it all quieted down back home. While the couple lived there, Paulin and his father would get into loud and sometimes physical fights. Eventually, this led to Paulin and Mathurin ending their relationship, and Mathurin returned to Paris.

Paulin stayed in town and began a business,

hiring transvestite artists and getting them jobs. Paulin's new company wouldn't make it a year, and he eventually returned to Paris as well in the Fall of 1985.

The attacks and robberies of older ladies in their homes began again in December 1985, and over the next six months, eight more women were murdered. The media picked up the news of the attacks, and the police presence became strong again.

It wasn't long before detectives connected the new murderer to the same murderer of the 1984 series of murders. The fingerprints of the murderer matched those of both series. The only significant difference police found in the two groups of murders was that the current murders weren't as cruel to the victims as the first set of murders were.

In the Fall of 1986, Paulin got into an argument with his cocaine dealer, which became physical. Paulin ended up beating him with a baseball bat. When the police arrived, the drug dealer told them who beat him, and Paulin was arrested. He was later charged and convicted of the assault and sentenced to sixteen months in prison. He only served twelve months and was released on good behavior.

During his time in prison, Paulin found out that he was HIV positive. Instead of quitting crime and drugs and trying to begin to live better in the time he had left, the news had the opposite effect. He decided that because he was sick, he had to kill as many people as he could before he died.

Once out of prison, Paulin returned to his criminal lifestyle. With the money and stolen credit cards he had earned from thefts, he had large parties and held different events, spending money like it was nothing.

To keep up with the fast pace he was living and spending, he started robing even more older ladies, sometimes even two robberies a day.

On November 25, 1987, he killed seventy-nine-year-old Rachel Cohen, and that same afternoon, he strangled eighty-seven-year-old Berthe Finalteri and robbed her. The very next morning, he murdered Geneviève Germont, who was ninety years old.

With all of the money Paulin got from these last three victims, he held a huge party celebrating his twenty-fourth birthday. Meanwhile, one of his victims, Finalteri, survived her attack. When Paulin choked her, she passed out, and he thought she was dead, but she wasn't. She gave detectives a good description of Pauline, and he was arrested on December 1st.

It only took Paulin two days in custody before he began confessing his crimes to the police. In total, detectives accused him of murdering eighteen people, but he admitted to having killed twenty-one victims. Paulin admitted to looking for his victims in stores, and he would talk to them while shopping. They would become one of his targets if he thought the lady was not very friendly or miserable. He would follow them to where they lived and scope out the place to see if they lived alone and if he could break in.

In the early part of 1988, Paulin became sick while in jail awaiting his trial. He was brought to the hospital in a state of paralysis, and later, it was determined that he had tuberculosis and meningitis, and by April 1989, he died.

Mathurin would later be tried for nine of the murders and robberies that happened in 1984, and he was convicted and sentenced to life imprisonment. He was released on parole in January 2009 after serving twenty years.

EIGHTEEN

Francis Heaulime

THE CRIMINAL BACKPACKER

Francis Heaulme was born in Metz, France, on February 25, 1959. It was said that his father was very abusive towards him, so much so that Francis attempted suicide when he was seventeen. He loved his mother and baby sister very much, though, but his mother died of cancer when he was twenty-three.

Heaulime started riding bikes as a teenager. By

the time he turned twenty, he was an advanced cyclist, which later led him to travel around France and the rest of Europe on his bike. He sometimes used the rail to travel and stayed in different shelters, fields, or parks.

Often, Heaulime picked up odd jobs for a short time to help pay for his traveling expenses and drinking alcohol. His inclination for drinking gradually worsened over time. He often checked himself into detox clinics or psychiatric hospitals to clear his head and get back on track again.

Heaulime also had Klinefelter's syndrome, which he never sought treatment for, which meant that he had an extra X chromosome. The illness usually results in infertility, making it not possible for him to commit rape or sexual assault in a typical way. The inability also contributed to his alcoholism.

Years later, Heaulime confessed to being present while a male friend of his raped two different women on two occasions, and Heaulime just watched until it was over. He then murdered the victim. During the times he was in psychiatric hospitals, he admitted his murders to the doctors. Still, they never took the confessions seriously since he was regularly confessing to crimes. The doctors figured they were just fantasies of his.

Heaulime was arrested on January 7, 1992, in Bischwiller. Police knew they had the right suspect in custody but had difficulty getting the evidence to ensure a conviction. One problem was that he didn't have the sexual means to rape the victims, and secondly, Heaulime had alibis for some of the crimes. Dozens of sexual assault and murder crimes were committed in 1987.

Eventually, Heaulime admitted to some of the crimes he committed. At times, he volunteered information about the sexual assault or murder and even agreed to take them to the scene and show them how it happened. The detectives knew he was clever and manipulative, so he couldn't always be trusted during the interviews. He would give them enough information to know that he was involved in the crime but not enough to convict him.

In Port-Grimaud, an eight-year-old, Jorris Viville, was raped and murdered. Detectives not only knew that he was unable to commit the rape, but the body of the girl was also moved over twenty kilometers by car, and Heaulime didn't drive. Police listed five suspects they believed it was, but Heaulime was too scared to give their names. In the end, he would be later convicted alone in this specific case and receive a life sentence for the crime.

Heaulime was linked to the sexual assault and murder of forty-four-year-old Aline Peres, who was killed on the beach in the middle of the day. Even with several other people on the beach that same afternoon, police could not find any witnesses. It would take four years for police to connect Heaulime to the crime and charge him with it. He alone would be convicted of this crime and given a twenty-year sentence in prison.

Police wanted to know who he was with while the crimes were happening, as they were the person who committed the actual sexual assault on the victim. Not very often did Heaulime give up the name of his accomplice. One crime where he gave up the other person was the crime that happened at the fair in the city of Metz.

While sitting at a bar having a drink, he started talking to another man beside him. After a few drinks, the man suggested that Heaulime come with him to visit his cousin, saying that it would be fun. The two men went to his cousin's house, Laurence Guillaume, who happened to be a fourteen-year-old girl. After they talked with the young girl for a while and made sure nobody else was at her house, the man sexually assaulted her.

After he was finished, he offered her up to Heaulime, who, instead of trying to have sex with her, strangled her to death. Heaulime admitted to the crime and gave the name of the man who raped her. His accomplice was convicted of rape and accessory to murder and given eighteen years in prison.

Heaulime is serving out his life in prison and is currently still alive.

NINETEEN

Francois Verove

LE GRELE (POCKMARKED MAN)

Francois Verove was born an only child in Gravelines, Nord, France, on January 22, 1962. Within two weeks of his birth, his mother died of the flu while still in the hospital. About a year later, his father married a divorced woman with two girls from her first marriage. It is said that he grew up becoming a fan of horror films.

Verove joined the police force in 1983 and

moved to Paris, where he would work as a motorcycle policeman for the National Police Force. In 1988, he switched to another national police force and worked for the Ministry of Interior. While working with both police forces, he was a delegate for the union and was well-liked during his police career.

Verove retired around 2019 and moved to Prades-le-Lez in southern France. He appeared on a French television game show that year. Also that year, he was elected to the city as one of their councilors. After serving two years as a counselor, he retired and moved to La Grande-Motte. When he was discovered for the crimes he had committed, he committed suicide.

Crimes

When an eight-year-old girl left her apartment in Paris on April 7, 1986, Verove entered the same elevator and began speaking to her. He suddenly grabbed the child and forced her into the basement of the building, where he raped her and strangled her. He fled the scene believing that she was dead, but she regained consciousness and went for help.

A month later, on May 5, 1986, Cecile Bloch,

an eleven-year-old girl, left her apartment to go to school. When she got onto the elevator in her apartment building, Verove was already on it, and the two rode down together. Like his first victim, he forced her to go to the basement of the building with him and took her to an empty room. There, he strangled her until she lost consciousness, then he sexually assaulted her. After he was finished, he wanted to make sure that she was dead, so he stabbed her several times. He stabbed her so violently that he broke her spine. Then, he wrapped her body in some old carpet and left her there.

The janitor of the building found the girl's body the following day. Police canvassed the whole building and learned about a strange man seen in and around the building that same morning. From their description, they could create a composite drawing of him. One key element they all mentioned was that the man had several acne marks on his face and later would be called "The Pockmarked Killer."

Now that there had been two victims within one month and a composite sketch was making the rounds on all media, the area became panicked. With nobody letting their children out alone and the police doubling their patrols, Verove decided to take a break from his attacks. He wouldn't strike again until almost a year later. He also decided to change who he targeted. From now on, he would only target a pair of adults instead of children.

On the afternoon of April 28, 1987, thirty-eight-year-old Gilles Politi, who worked as a technician, and Irmgard Muller, his German au pair who took care of his children, were found dead in the Politi apartment located in the Marais district of Paris. Both bodies were stripped naked. Politi had been strangled and was lying face down on a bedroom floor with his hands and feet tied behind his back. Muller was also in the bedroom, but she was hanging by her arms from an upright bed frame with her throat cut by a knife. Both victims had been tortured with cigarette burns all over their bodies.

Police found one significant lead in Muller's personal phone book. Elie Lauringe, one of her contacts with whom she seemed to be having a relationship, was listed. But when the police looked for the name in the directory, it didn't exist. The police believed that it was not a real name. When police canvased the apartment building, several neighbors said that they had seen a twenty-something-year-old athletic-looking man go into the apartment the day before the bodies were found. Another witness claimed to have heard the same man speaking to Muller over the intercom the morning of the murders.

Again, terror took hold of the city. The new murders were on everyone's minds, but they were not connected to the young girl's attacks from the year before because the victims were so different.

In the Fall of the same year, on October 27th, Verove spotted a fourteen-year-old girl walking down the street on her way home from school. He stopped her and said that he was a police officer and that he needed to ask her some questions. He took her into an apartment, where he handcuffed her and then sexually assaulted her. Verove then ransacked the apartment, removed some money and valuables, and left the girl alive, still cuffed to the bed. This attack was the last known attack from Verove for seven years.

Ingrid G. was riding her bike along a railway line in Mitry-Mory, Seine-et-Marne when suddenly Verove pulled his car over in front of her. He claimed to be a police officer and that she needed to get in his vehicle. He was going to take her to the police station. Ingrid got into his car, and he drove away. He took her over an hour away to an abandoned farm in Saclay, Essonne.

Once they arrived there, he tied her up and raped her for several hours before leaving. Again, like with his last victim, he didn't kill her but just left.

Detectives started to think that the killer might also be a policeman as he used handcuffs and a walkie-talkie as police officers do. Also, with the last two victims, he said he was an officer and showed them an official police business card to convince his victims to come with him. The survivors also described the way their attacker had spoken to them, and he used several common police sayings while he was with them.

The lead investigator ordered a DNA sample from the seven hundred and fifty officers who had been on active duty in the areas of the crimes in 2021. When Verove received the phone call asking him to come into police headquarters to give his blood sample, he said he would. But after hanging up the phone, he wrote a suicide note and left it for his wife.

In the note, Verove claimed that he had committed several unforgivable acts on other people until the late nineties. These violent acts that Verove was admitting to, he also claimed, only happened due to him suffering from uncontrollable impulses that he couldn't always control.

Two days after Verove's body was found, detectives took his blood sample, and his DNA matched the profile of the murderer on all of the crime scenes where police had a DNA sample of the attacker.

Verove's DNA sample also connected him to two other murders. Twenty-three-year-old realtor Sophie Name was murdered in an apartment that she had been showing on December 5, 1991. Also, on June 9, 1994, nineteen-year-old Karine Leroy vanished from her home. Her body was discovered a month later in a nearby park.

TWENTY

Michel Fourniret

OGRE OF THE ARDENNES

Michel Paul Fourniret was born in Sedan, France, on April 4, 1942. His father was an ironworker, and his mother was a stay-at-home parent. He loved listening to classical music and playing chess and was a deep thinker who seldom talked with others. After he was arrested years later, during an interview with detectives, he claimed that his mother had sexually abused him from a very young age.

After he finished schooling, Fourniret got a job with the government's forestry department and moved away from home. He didn't stay long at that job and went from job to job over the next few years. Most of the jobs involved labor or construction, and he worked for the school. Eventually, he became a supervisor there.

While at the school, Fourinet was arrested for sexually assaulting a young student. He served less than two years before being released. After jail, he moved back home and started doing menial jobs again.

In 1984, he was arrested again for sexual assault. He had five charges against him this time, so when he was convicted, he was sentenced to five years. During his time in prison, he started using the prison pen pal system and became acquainted with Monique Olivier. During their correspondence, he told her about his desires and fantasies of raping young girls who were still virgins. She responded to him that she would help him to live out his dreams when he was released, but only if he would murder her husband.

Fourinet was released in 1987, and the two met and began a relationship. It wasn't long after that when the couple started to go out and find young girls for him to rape. She held up her part of the deal as an accomplice, but he never did murder her husband for her.

The couple would go to a specific part of town to search for possible victims. In December 1987, they chose to go to Auxerre, and it was there that they noticed Isabelle Laville, a seventeen-year-old student, walking home from school alone. They followed her until she got to her home. They left and returned the following day around the same time to wait for Laville, and they followed her until she got home.

Finally, on December 11th, they drove back to Auxerre again, but they each went in separate cars this time. When they saw Laville walking the same route she had on the previous days, Olivier followed her in her car. A few blocks down the road, she pulled her car over in front of Laville, opened her window, and said she was lost and needed help. Laville said she'd be glad to help her and got into the passenger side of her car.

Fourniret had driven his car further down the road towards Laville's house and parked. He got out of his car, opened the hood, stood there looking at the engine, and waited for Olivier to arrive with Laville. When Olivier pulled up beside Fourniret and stopped her car, she asked him what was wrong. He claimed he didn't know, so Olivier offered him a ride to a service station to get help. He agreed and hopped into the back seat of her car.

From the back seat, Fourniret took a small rope that he had in his pocket and choked Laville. Olivier then drove the three of them back to their place in Saint-Cyr-les-Clons. They both carried Laville upstairs into their bedroom, where Fourniret raped her. After he was finished, he choked her to death with his bare hands. He then put Laville's body back in the car and took her to a different town, where he threw her body into the well of an abandoned home. Laville's body wouldn't be found for almost eighteen years.

Back when Fourniret was in prison, he shared his cell with a bank robber, Jean-Pierre Hellegouarch, who told Fourniret about a robbery he had been involved in where his gang had stolen a million francs worth of gold and coins. Hellegouarch also knew where it was hidden and told Fourniret that if he could help his wife retrieve the gold, they would give him half of it. He agreed to help.

So in March 1988, Hellegouarch's wife, Farida, contacted Fourniret, and they made plans to meet and get the gold. They went where the gold was, dug it up, returned to Farida's apartment, split the stash, and Fourniret left.

Later, Fourniret and Olivier decided they should also steal Farida's half of the gold, so they called her up and planned to go out for lunch on April 12th. After they finished lunch, the three of them decided to go for a drive through the park. Once they found an isolated spot, Fourniret strangled Farida to death. They then took the body and buried it before returning to her apartment to steal her gold. Farida's body was never found.

Even though Olivier was pregnant with Fourniret's child, they continued to look for victims for him to assault and murder sexually. On August 3rd, they waited in a grocery store parking lot for a single woman to park in the lot on her way shopping. It wasn't long before Fabienne Leroy drove up beside them and parked.

Olivier got out of their car and pretended to faint. Both Fourniret and Leroy ran to check on her. The couple asked if she knew where there was a hospital that they could go to as they didn't know the area. Leroy jumped in their car to show them how to get there. Fourniret instead drove her to an isolated area where there was a forest. He raped her and then shot her in the chest. They buried Leroy in the woods and left.

One afternoon in January 1989, when Fourniret was taking the train, he began talking with a young woman, Jeanne-Marie Desramault, who was on her way home where she lived in a convent in Mezieres. They got along well and exchanged phone numbers. They talked a few times again over the next month. In one of those conversations, they planned to meet so that Deseramault could meet his wife, Monique, and have lunch at their house.

On March 16th, the three met at the same train station and traveled to Fourniret and Olivier's house. He promised to drive her home later so she didn't have to take the train. After getting to their house, they sat, had a drink, and talked. Fourniret asked Desramault if she was still a virgin before she was at the convent. She told him that she wasn't a virgin and had a regular boyfriend. The admission made him so angry that he began to slap her. She hit him back, which made him even more furious. So he jumped on her and strangled her to death. They took her body out to the Chateau du Sautou and buried it in their gardens.

Fourniret and Olivier married in July, and their first child, a boy, was born. By the Fall of that year, the couple was out looking for new victims. They traveled to Saint-Servais, Namur, on the afternoon of December 20, 1989, and brought their baby. While driving the neighborhood, Fourniret saw twelve-year-old Elisabeth Brichet walking alone to her friend's house. They followed her there, parked outside the house across the street, and waited for her to leave.

Shortly before 6:30 that evening, Brichet left and started to walk back towards her home. They drove past her slowly and stopped. Fourniret asked her if she knew where the hospital was, as they needed to see a doctor and weren't familiar with the area. Brichet got into their car and started to tell them directions.

Somehow, they got Brichet to go back to their house. Once there, Fourniret stripped the girl naked and noticed that she was menstruating. Olivier had to tend to the girl and clean her up. The following day, Fourniret sexually assaulted her and, afterward, put a plastic bag over her head to kill her. For some reason, he couldn't kill her with the bag, so he choked her with his bare hands. They took her body and buried it close to one of their other victims. Her body wasn't discovered until the Summer of 2004 after the couple were arrested and confessed to killing her.

Fourniret and Olivier committed their last murder in November 1990. The couple drove their new white van to a shopping mall in Reze and parked there. Shortly after parking, they noticed thirteen-year-old Natacha Danais cutting through the parking lot and walking by their car. Olivier jumped out and asked for directions, and Danais agreed to go with them to show them where they wanted to go.

Instead, the couple took her to a quiet part of the local park, where he undressed and raped her before stabbing her to death with a screwdriver. They drove to the beach, dumped her body there, and then returned home. The following morning, police found the body and started to canvas the beach for any possible witnesses. Several people had seen Danais enter a white van in the shopping mall parking lot. Police also determined that Danais was also sexually assaulted after she was murdered.

About a week later, police arrested Danais' next-door neighbor, Jean Groix, mainly because he had owned a white van, like the one seen picking up Danais at the mall. When police searched Groix's house, they found several members of the ETA, a separationist group who had been hiding out there. Detectives then thought that perhaps Danais had discovered this and, therefore, Groix murdered her. Groix would kill himself while in his cell two months later.

In 1991, Fourniret and Olivier moved to Sart-Custinne, Gedinne, Belgium. It was over nine years before he would kill again. In May 2000, Fourniret was driving to Charleville-Mezieres when he saw an eighteen-year-old student walking home alone. Somehow he lured her into his van, and he raped her, strangled her with a rope, and drove her body back to Belgium before dumping her in the forest in Sugny, Vresse-sur-Semois. A few months later, some mushroom pickers found her body in July.

Fourniret headed back to Sedan on May 5, 2001, to pick up Mananya Thumpong, a thirteen-year-old girl from Thailand, whom he had met several weeks before at the library. He was taking her back to his house so she could look after his son for a while. Instead of taking her back home, he took her to Nollevaux, Paliseul, where he strangled her and dumped her remains in a park.

Her remains were found almost a year later, on March 1, 2002, half eaten by wild animals.

On June 26, 2003, the police went to Fourniret's home in Belgium and arrested him after a failed attempt to abduct a thirteen-year-old girl from a parking lot. They also arrested Olivier as well. After several hours of interrogations on both of them, the police learned nothing and were forced to let them go.

In 2004, Olivier told detectives that her husband had murdered several people over the years since 1987. Police arrested Fourniret again, and this time, during their interviews with him, he confessed to murdering eight different women between the ages of twelve and thirty years old and a man whom he wasn't sure of the age. Four of the victims whom he confessed to murdering were discovered all in France.

Police would also arrest Olivier for being an accessory to several of the murders, and the couple was deported back to France. The couple ended up helping police find three more of their victims before standing trial for murder, which started on March 27, 2008.

The trial lasted two months, ending with Fourniret being found guilty of seven murders. He was sentenced to life in prison without any chance of parole. Olivier was found guilty of being an accessory to seven murders and sentenced to life in prison without the possibility of parole for twenty-eight years. The couple was also fined a half million francs to the victims' family members as compensation. Neither Olivier nor Fourniret appealed their convictions. In one of the murder cases that Fourniret was charged with, he was acquitted because there wasn't enough evidence present.

On July 2, 2010, the couple had a quiet divorce granted by the family court in Charleville-Mezieres. Olivier first applied for it because she no longer wanted to have any contact with him. Fournirct agreed to the divorce without any challenge.

Ten years after the trial, in 2018, Fourniret confessed to police that he had also murdered two other women: eighteen-year-old Marie-Angele Domerce, who was disabled in the Summer of 1988, and twenty-year-old Joanna Parrish, in May 1990. A few years after that confession, in March 2020, he confessed to murdering another woman who had gone missing in January 2003, Estelle Mouzin.

Fourniret died in the hospital at the age of seventy-nine from respiratory issues on May 10,

2021. He had left everything he owned to his son, Selim, including a life insurance policy. Because he only had 50,000 francs in the bank at the time of his conviction, which wasn't nearly enough to pay the fine he still owed the court, they seized the life insurance policy, leaving Selim nothing.

TWENTY-ONE

Yvan Keller

THE PILLOW KILLER

Yvan Keller was born in Wittenheim, Haut-Rhin, France, on December 13, 1960. His parents were what is known as passive travelers. They would go somewhere and stay there for an extended period before moving again. Yvan had seven siblings who lived together in a small place, and his parents didn't make much money. His father worked in a mine, and his mother made baskets to sell. As soon as Yvan was old enough to work, his father made him go out and get a job to help support the family. Soon after he quit school and started working, his mother died. She was only forty-nine.

When Yvan turned seventeen in 1981, he was caught stealing some antique pieces from a dealer in Battenheim. He was arrested, tried, and convicted of robbery. He was sentenced to serve ten years in prison. He was released after eight years in August 1989.

After prison, he moved to the suburbs, lived in a one-room apartment, and worked as a landscaper. He was good at it, and his popularity grew, so he created his own company, Alsa-Jardin. As the company expanded, he began living a better lifestyle. His neighbors liked him.

While living in the apartment, he met Marina, and after dating for a short while, she moved in with him. But it was short-lived. After only about six months, she moved out because, according to her, Yvan lived beyond their means. He would go to the casino and spend all of his money on drinks and gambling. When he ended up short on cash, he would make her prostitute herself and take the money she made.

After Marina left Yvan, he began dating another woman, Séverine, who refused to move in with him. Later, he found out that she was seeing another man, which was why she wouldn't commit to him. He forced Séverine to tell him where this other man lived. He took his gun and threatened him to leave her, or he would kill him.

In January 1994, Marie Winterhoer was found dead in her bed, lying face up. After an autopsy was performed, it was ruled that her death was from natural causes. Two months later, on March 12, 1994, when a man went to visit his mother, eight-six-year-old Ernestine Mang, he found her dead lying in her bed. Oddly, an old butter churn was in her room. Something that was usually kept in the cellar. It was surprising to see it there since his mother had terrible arthritis and could hardly move much, never mind dragging the butter churn upstairs from the basement.

Just over a month after that, on April 27th, Augusta Wassmer was found dead, lying face up in her bed by her daughter, Marie-Francoise Roecklin. Wassmer's bank card was taken and used three times to take cash out of the account.

Later, the autopsy said that she had died from cardiac arrest.

Police had looked at Keller two times as a possible suspect because he seemed to have had some connection with the victims, but there was no evidence to arrest him. The police brought him in for questioning regardless. Eventually, he confessed to having murdered around one hundred and fifty people in all.

Whenever Keller got a landscaping job, and his customer was an older person living alone, he would check out what things they owned in the house. If it looked like there were things of value, he would murder them and then rob their house. Keller would also make it look as though his victims had died from natural causes by suffocating them in their beds. Keller would sell off his victim's items to different thrift shops.

After his arrest and awaiting to stand trial, Keller hung himself in his cell using his shoelaces tied around a light fixture.

TWENTY-TWO

Remy Roy

THE MINTIER KILLER

R emy Roy was born in an undetermined part of France sometime in 1958. Growing up, he attended the Brothers of Saint-Vincent de Paul religious school. After graduating, he attended a school to learn how to sail a boat and became a sea captain. He became popular in the yachting community and met a bookstore owner whom he dated and married. The couple bought a house in Villejuif and had two children.

At first, Roy helped run his new wife's bookstore, but in 1988, she hired a friend to help her, leaving Roy looking for something else to do. He opened a promotional video company, but it failed. After it closed, he began to stay at home a lot and spent most of his time sleeping, watching television, and eating. Over the next year, he gained a lot of weight, weighing over two hundred and twenty pounds.

During this time, Roy began to use the Minitel service, a new service to meet other people over the phone. It was one of the first services where people could send other people videos, usually to have sex with each other. The service became popular amongst BDSM and other erotic sex groups at the time.

After a few years, Roy planned to meet others on the Minitel service. His first meeting was with Paul Bernard, a forty-six-year-old insurance salesman. They set the afternoon of October 11, 1990, as the date they would meet on the Seine River at a marina in Daveil. Bernard was living with his mother at her house in Issey-les-Moulineaux. He was already retired. He had been married years before, but his wife had passed from cancer.

Bernard liked being tied up and controlled during sex and had met up with other men through the Minitel before without any issues. After the two men met, they went to an isolated part of the river. There, Bernard allowed Roy to tie his hand behind his back, wrap a scarf around his face, and tie a string around his testicles. But instead of engaging in sexual activity, Roy was slowly suffocating Bernard. Then he picked up a large rock and crushed his head with it.

The following day, a fisherman came across Bernard's body lying completely naked on the shore, except for a pair of pants covering his face. The medical examiner determined that Bernard had died from asphyxia and had found what looked like tie marks around his neck. Bernard's car was found in a parking lot a kilometer away from where his body had been located.

Roy's subsequent encounter with the Minitel service was on the night of October 19, 1990. He met a man calling himself Gilbert Duquesnoy at a coffee shop. Roy learned that the man was an astrologer called "Nathaniel the Magician."

After a few coffees, the two went to Duquesnoy's

office, where they had a few glasses of port. Once they were both comfortable, Roy placed a leather mask over Duquesnoy's head and tied his hands and feet behind his back. Roy then pulled a hammer that he had brought with him out of a duffle bag and began to strike Duquesoy over the head. He hit him at least seven or eight times. Once he lost consciousness, Roy looked for and found Duquesnoy's diary and address book before quickly leaving the building. Walking by the Marne River, he threw his hammer into it, took the diary and address book to a train station, and left it on the platform.

Duquesnoy's partner, Alain, was getting no answer for two days when he called his office. Alain had two of Duquesnoy's neighbors go to his office to see if he was there. When the neighbors went into the suite, they found Duquesnoy lying naked with an opened briefcase beside him containing several sex toys. The place was a mess, with several items knocked over as it looked like he had been robbed.

Roy's next meeting was with a forty-one-year-old construction manager, Hugues Moreau, whom he also met on Minitel, and the two decided to meet at Moreau's house at eleven in the morning on November 17, 1990. Moreau asked to be tied up while lying naked on his bed. Soon after that,

Roy grabbed a steel pipe and beat Moreau to death with it, then he ransacked the house and stole a fax machine, checkbooks, and a bank card that he found. Moreau's wife returned later that day after she finished work and saw him lying naked on the bed with a pile of sex toys beside him.

Roy wouldn't meet anybody for almost another year. On October 8, 1991, he set up a date with Bruno Giraudon, a thirty-two-year-old civil servant living in Villeneuve-Saint-Georges. The two went for drinks at Giraudon's house, and while talking, Roy told Giraudon that he was a photographer who worked in the sailing world and was good at sadomasochistic play. He opened up the duffle bag that he had with him and showed Giraudon some sex toys that he had brought with him. He then asked if he wanted to try some of them, but Giraudon refused.

Surprised by the response, Roy grabbed a lamp from an end table and hit Giraudon over his head, and he passed out. Roy then went through his house and took his identification and checkbook. Roy also left his sex toys behind when he fled the house. Giraudon's friends looked for him the next day, and they found him in his home, alive but unconscious, covered in blood, and naked. They took him to the hospital, and he recovered from his injuries. He gave the police a good description of his attacker.

In November, Roy went to an electronics store, and while talking to a salesman, he claimed that he made underwater films with his camcorder and needed a VCR and Video editor. The price was 14,000 francs, which he paid for with one of his victims' stolen checks. However, because the check was for such a large amount of money, the store required him to show his identification. Roy showed them his identification without remembering that the name on the check was different. Lucky for Roy, the salesman didn't notice either.

A few hours later, Roy went to another electronics store to buy more things he needed. Again, he paid with one of his victims' checks while using his identification. Again, the store salesman didn't notice that the name on the check was different from his identification. The second store had a surveillance camera, though, and was recording Roy's time there.

Later, after detectives learned that one of the victim's checks had been used in the store, they went there to speak to the sales clerks to see what they remembered. They got the camera footage showing Roy in the store. Then, they released still shots of Roy to the media. Soon after that, he was identified, and on November 28, 1991, he was arrested.

Police then made a complete search of Roy's home, and there they found more of his victims' checkbooks and driver's licenses. After being confronted with this evidence, Roy confessed to doing the recent murders and robberies. When he was asked if he was homosexual, Roy denied it, claiming that he hated gay men.

Later, he told a psychiatrist about some of his experiences as a young boy that caused him to hate gay men. While Roy was only about ten years old, some of his classmates forced him into the woods, where they removed all of his clothing, tied him to a tree, and made fun of him. Also, when he was thirteen, he was in a movie theatre watching a film when a man who was sitting beside him masturbated and ejaculated on him. But the most terrifying thing that happened to Roy was when he was seventeen and working as a repairman for an electronics store. While on a service call for a group of men, they accused him of charging them too much for his work and wanted some money paid back to them. When he didn't have enough to pay them, he ran. The men later came after him, and when they found him, Roy claimed that they gang-raped him. Police investigated all of these events that Roy had claimed had happened to him but found no evidence of any of them happening. Instead, they turned out to be false memories that Roy had.

After police completed their investigation on Roy, he was charged with two counts of murder, one count of manslaughter, and one count of attempted murder. His trial started on June 26, 1996, and only lasted for two days before he was convicted of all charges and sentenced to life imprisonment.

TWENTY-THREE

Guy Georges

THE BEAST OF THE BASTILLE

Guy Georges, born Guy Rampillion, was born in Vitry-le-Francois, France, on October 15, 1962. His father was an African-American, George Cartwright, who worked as a cook on a NATO base. His mother,

Helène Rampillon, was a French woman who already had another son, Stéphane, with a different U.S. soldier.

Even though Helène's parents helped raise Stéphane, they could not raise Guy, partly because of where they lived, Angers. He would have been stigmatized as a mixed-race child. In 1968, Guy's last name was changed to "Georges" after his birth father's first name. Also in 1968, Helène moved to California, United States, and took her older son. She had hoped to marry a U.S. soldier.

After his mother and brother left France, Guy went into foster care and was a ward of the state. Eventually, he was placed with the Morin family, who already had twenty children to look after. Thirteen were adopted, and seven were their biological children.

As a child, he began to steal things from stores, including money and food. When he was robbing places, he always showed a knife, and he would use the nickname "Injun Joe" after *The Adventures of Tom Sawyer*.

When Guy turned fourteen in 1976, he tried strangling his younger foster sister, Roselyne, who was mentally disabled. A couple of years later, in 1978, he tried strangling another foster sister,

Christiane. She testified that he tried to strangle her with an iron bar from a weightlifting set.

The family called the police, and Guy was sent to a state orphanage group home shortly after that, where he could have an eye kept on him.

Even from his new home, he continued to commit crimes such as assaults and robberies. He continued attacking, raping, and trying to kill women until his first successful murder in 1991.

From the years 1991 to 1997, Guy assaulted, tortured, raped, and killed seven women in the neighborhood of the Bastille, the Bourbon-era Parisian prison.

Guy was finally arrested on March 26, 1998, after a DNA comparison, and readily admitted his guilt to the police during interrogation. He was diagnosed as a "narcissistic psychopath" by the psychiatrists who treated him.

In April 2001, Guy was tried and sentenced to life imprisonment without the possibility of parole for 22 years.

TWENTY-FOUR

Honoré Zanchi

THE AVENGER

Honoré Zanchi was born in Aiguèze, France, on May 4, 1962. He lived in Aiguèze for the first seven years with his three other siblings and loved living there. Then, the family moved to Annonay in 1969. The move was hard on him; he began committing small thefts afterward. It was assumed his behavior was more about attracting attention to himself than the small items he stole, which he had no interest in. As he got older, he began to take things from grocery stores or corner convenience stores, usually food or drink.

In 1977, at fifteen, Honoré quit school to work as a laborer. By 1978, he worked as a bricklayer but still did not make enough money to live like he wanted. So, he continued to steal to fill in where his salary couldn't. His thefts became larger, and instead of just taking food or drinks, he started holding up the stores and taking their money. By the end of the year, he tried to rob a theater in Annonay, but he was caught and arrested. He was given a two-year prison sentence, but after serving one year, they released him with six months of probation.

In the early 1980s, Honoré met Jean-François André, who was part of the motorcycle subculture and rode a Harley-Davidson. The two men became like brothers and did everything together, including thefts. Honoré was caught and arrested several times but served no time for his crimes.

André opened a bar in Drôme in 1985 for bikers and their enthusiasts. Even though Honoré kept getting into minor legal troubles, the two remained good friends. The police watched the bar that André owned closely as they suspected drugs were being sold there, but there were never any raids or arrests.

In 1990, the woman Honoré was dating had a baby boy, Angelino, for him.

One night in February 1992, a biker and good friend of Honoré's was beaten up by another man Honoré knew but wasn't friends with. After learning of the assault, Honoré bought two 9 mm. guns without getting a license and decided that he would go after the man who attacked his friend.

On February 23rd, Honoré found the man he sought in a restaurant in Saint-Rambert-d'Albon. He walked in, pulled out one of his guns, and shot the man several times until he was dead. Instead of running, he went to the closest police station and told them what he had done. The police arrested him and placed him in jail. He defended his actions to the police by saying that he only shot the man because the man had beaten up his friend for no reason. Honoré was charged with having an unlicensed gun and murder.

During his trial in 1996, several members of the community, friends, family, and even the man he had murdered for all testified to what a good man he was. They all believed that Honoré was justified in his actions. His vigilante justice did not sway the court. He ended up being convicted of manslaughter and was given a ten-year sentence for the crime of murder. For carrying an unlicensed weapon and being a convicted felon, he got an additional two-year sentence.

In January 2000, Honoré was released from prison on parole and moved in with his girlfriend and son. When he returned to André's bar, everyone treated him like a celebrity for what he had done.

Later that year, on November 2nd, Honoré and his girlfriend had twin boys, Enzo and Gino, which made him decide to quit committing crimes, get a proper job, and care for his family. It was short-lived. In the Summer of 2002, Honoré was caught trying to burglarize a corner store and arrested. He was given a seven-month sentence and released the following January 2003.

Just before Honoré was released from jail, his best friend, André, was murdered outside of his home. He was only forty-two. When he got out of prison, Honoré was devastated and blamed himself for not being around as he might have been able to help André, and he might still be alive. In December 2003, the biker community held a large funeral for André, including thousands of bikers from around North America.

Police were never able to find out who

murdered André. They questioned over one hundred different people from the community, but nothing. The two main suspects were Michel Di Bacco and Gerald Crouzet.

In May 2004, Honoré was arrested for committing another burglary, this time of a house. He was also carrying a gun. He was convicted on both charges and sentenced to another fifteen months in prison. He was released in 2006 but committed another robbery and was convicted again, this time getting a thirty-month sentence of imprisonment. Again, he was released early for good behavior and placed on parole in late 2006.

Honoré was still seeking revenge on Di Bacco and Crouzet for the murder of his friend André. He decided that he would break into a gun shop, steal some weapons, then use them to kill the two men. As he was fleeing from the gun shop, he was caught by police and arrested. Honoré would receive another thirty-month prison sentence for the gun shop burglary. By the time he was released in late April 2008, he was hell-bent on killing the two men he thought killed André. It was all he could think about.

While driving around the town on May 13, 2008, Honoré saw Crouzet driving his Mercedes, so he followed him. Once he had the chance, he surprised Crouzet and made him drive off the road and into a ditch. Honoré quickly jumped out of his car and climbed into Crouzet's car, where he shot him in the head and killed him. Police found Crouzet dead in his car later that same day. For some reason, the medical examiner ruled his death was due to a heart attack. The investigation was closed, and the man was buried.

Near the end of July 2008, Honoré drove to the bar where Di Bacco often went to drink and hang out. When he saw his car parked out front, he parked across the street and waited for Di Bacco to leave. After the bar closed and Di Bacco staggered towards his vehicle, Honoré got out of his car, walked up to him, and shot him thirteen times, killing him before leaving the scene.

Police launched a full investigation into the murder and canvased everyone who was around that bar during that night, as well as the employees and all of the victim's friends and family they could find. Most of the witnesses and people who knew the victim thought that there was probably a connection between Di Bacco's murder and the death of Crouzet. They also believed that there was some relationship between the killings and the murder of André years before. But there wasn't any evidence to lead to a suspect.

Detectives decided to take another look at Crouzet's death and exhumed his body. This time, the medical examiner discovered the gunshot wound to the head and changed his ruling of Crouzet's death to homicide. Knowing about Honoré's criminal past and friendship with André, he was now their primary suspect in both murders. Police began watching Honoré by having undercover officers follow him everywhere he went. They also wiretapped his house, looking for any evidence to arrest him, but none of that worked.

The following Spring, on March 25, 2009, Honoré ran into Di Bacco's best friend, Marc Nepote-Cit, a thirty-five-year-old car mechanic. The two got into a fight, which resulted in Honoré shooting Nepote-Cit to death. He then dumped the body near the Roche Pereandre.

After this murder, Honoré bragged about the killings of the three men to everyone around the bars who would listen. Eventually, the stories got around to the police, who brought him in for questioning on April 27, 2009.

While Honoré was being interrogated, he told police that he was the "Great Avenger" and one of the best when it comes to shooting his gun. But he denied being involved in any of the murders. The following day after Honoré was arrested, police brought in twenty-one more men for questioning. Three days later, feeling under pressure from a lot of his friends being held in jail, he finally admitted that he was involved in the murders. He was formerly charged with the three murders, and all the others were released.

Honoré's trial began on September 18, 2012, in Drôme. Throughout the trial, he refused to explain the murders in detail or his motives for committing them. He was supported by many in the biker community, along with his girlfriend and André's family. Despite the support, the jury convicted him of two murders and one count of manslaughter in the Nepote-Cit death. He was sentenced to life imprisonment.

Honoré filed an appeal to his sentence, which was heard on March 25, 2014. The appeal trial lasted three days, and on March 28th, they found him guilty again on all three counts. But this time, the court found mitigating circumstances and commuted his sentence to only thirty years instead of life. He filed another appeal in 2015, but it was dismissed.

TWENTY-FIVE

Louis Poirson

RAMBO

L ouis Poirson was born in Madagascar sometime in September 1962. He was the oldest of four, with three younger sisters. His father was French, and his mother was Malagasy. While he was growing up, he was often ridiculed and beaten by his alcoholic father, while his mother just watched on and said nothing. Over the years, every time his father hit him, he started to hate his parents more and more. Despite the abuse, he was doing well at school, with good marks, and everyone seemed to like him.

After graduating from school, he started to work for a company that sailed people up and down the Rhine River, and his employer loved him. He was known for his strength, so in 1982, he wanted to become a paratrooper or commando in the army. But because he had a leg bone fracture, they wouldn't accept him. With conscription being the law, Poirson still had to join the military, but it wasn't how he had hoped.

Once Poirson finished his military service in the latter part of 1983, he returned to work boating people around.

Between 1983 and 1984, he committed seven sexual assaults. When he attacked the women, he would either hold a knife to their throats or choke them until they were unconscious before raping them.

In January 1985, Poirson was caught when his final victim saw his license plate number and was able to give it to the police. He was arrested and held in jail until his trial in December 1985. He was convicted of all seven charges of rape and assault and sentenced to a fifteen-year sentence in prison.

While serving his prison sentence, he joined their pen pal program and met Chantal Vaslet, a thirty-seven-year-old single mother of six girls. They continued to write to each other until he was released in July 1994 after only serving nine and one-half years. Once released, Poirson moved to Paris and worked as a stonemason.

On a sunny afternoon in August 1995, when Poirson had a day off, he decided to relax on the balcony of a neighboring bar and have a drink or two. While he was trying to enjoy his drink, a dog that was outside of a nearby house was continuously barking. As the dog barked, he became increasingly angry and left the bar.

Instead of trying to find the particular dog that kept barking, he walked to an animal cemetery. He walked to the caretaker's toolshed, broke into it, and grabbed a hammer. Then, he started to go through all the different animals' graves and trashed them.

While Poirson was doing this, two women, Jeanine Villain, sixty-seven, and her daughter, Monique, forty-four, went to the cemetery to visit the grave of one of their long-time dogs, Babette. When the two heard noises that sounded like things being broken, they went to find out what the noise was. They found Poirson smashing up the graves.

Monique began to yell at him and threatened to call the police. Poirson quickly pulled a knife out of his jacket and told them both to get into their car. He drove them to an isolated field and said he would let them go if they promised not to tell anyone, but Monique refused. Angry, Poirson hit her with his closed fist, knocking her out. Then he grabbed a plastic bag, put it over her head, and suffocated her to death. Jeanine got out of the car and began to run, but once he was sure that Monique was dead, Poirson got out and chased her down. When he caught up to her, Poirson threw his whole body weight at her, knocking her to the ground. Laying on top of her, he grabbed a piece of wood and beat her on the head until she stopped moving. He found a container with some gas in it, set the car on fire, and left the scene. Their bodies were found a few days later, but Poirson was never a suspect.

In June 1996, Louis Poirson kidnapped three 15-year-old hitchhikers and sequestrated them on the farm, but they escaped. He was arrested, tried in January 1997, and sentenced to three years in prison. He was released in July 1998.

On April 28, 1999, 73-year-old Lucie Pham-Ngoc-Bich went out for a walk as she did every day. Poirson, driving his wife's car, passed her and offered to give her a drive. She accepted. Soon after, she asked him to stop because she wanted to urinate. He stopped the car in a rest area and got out of the car to help her. He realized that she had relieved herself in her passenger seat. He was furious. He pushed her, and she fell. He put her back in the car and took her to the farm where he worked. Once there, he strangled her, then carried her body behind the farm to the edge of the field and buried it.

On September 5, 1999, Charlotte Berson, a seventy-nine-year-old widow who walked daily around the neighborhood, was seen by Poirson while driving by. He pulled over and stopped in front of her, blocking her passage. He opened his window and asked her if she needed a ride somewhere. She said no and asked him to move his car out of the way. She slapped the hood of his car. Poirson got angry. He got out of his vehicle and aggressively pushed her onto the ground, where she hit her head and passed out. He then picked her up, placed her into the backseat of the car, and drove to a park where he strangled her and hid her dead body in the bush. Before he left, he poured hydrochloric acid on her face and both hands, hoping to conceal her identity.

A month later, on October 3rd, a couple of hunters were walking through the park and came across her remains. She was wearing nothing except her watch. The police confirmed Berson's identity, as years before, she had a pin with a serial number on her watch. The family had reported Berson missing, and when police called them to identify her, they recognized her watch.

On May 3, 2000, Clémence, thirty-eight, accidentally took the wrong train from Paris when she went home. Once she realized it, she got off the train and walked to the bus stop. She was panicked because she was supposed to be at her son's school to watch him in a play. While she was sitting at the bus stop, Poirson happened to drive by. When he noticed she was alone, he asked her if she wanted a ride. He told her he had to drop off some boxes at his work before dropping her off. She accepted.

Once they arrived at his farm, he got out of the car, opened the trunk, and armed himself with a knife. He walked over to the passenger door, opened it, pointed the knife at her face, and told her to get out of the car. She got out of the car and began screaming. He hit her in the face, and she fell. He jumped on her, tied her hands behind her back, and dragged her inside the farmhouse and into a small room where there was a mattress lying on the floor. He threw her onto the bed, tied her up securely, and gagged her. He left her there and went to work in his studio. When he was dragging her into the house, her watch fell off and onto the front stairway.

Shortly after, Poirson's boss showed up at his farm, and as she entered the house, she saw a women's watch. She picked up the watch and continued into the house. Once inside the house, she heard a muffled noise coming from downstairs, so she decided to walk down the stairs to see if she could figure out what it was. As she walked by a closed bedroom door, she could hear the muffling sound coming from inside that room. She opened the door and saw a woman tied up and gagged and moaning.

Poirson suddenly noticed that his boss' car was parked in the driveway, and he dropped everything and ran down the stairs to find her. That's when he realized that his boss had gone downstairs and was in the room where he left Clémence. He walked slowly down the stairs until he reached the room and looked in.

His boss turned around and screamed at him,

wanting to know what was happening. He began apologizing to her and walked over to Clémence, where he slowly untied her and said he would take her home. He helped Clémence up the stairs, got into his car, and drove away. He drove Clémence to her home, apologized, and returned to the farm.

When he got to the farm, several police officers were waiting for him. His boss had called them and told them what he had done. He surrendered to the officers without incident. He was taken to the Bois d'Arcy prison and officially charged with kidnapping.

While investigators interrogated Poirson, he was very passive and calm. He never got loud and was very polite. He never admitted to any crime unless he was shown direct evidence.

Poirson got scared when detectives told him that because he had committed several of the crimes while he was driving his wife's car, they could arrest her for being an accessory to the crimes. He didn't want anything to happen to his wife, so he told them he would confess everything to them if they promised to leave her alone.

When police searched his home, they found several pieces of jewelry that didn't belong to his wife, so they took it to the station. They had several of the victim's families come and see if they could recognize any of them. Some of the jewelry was identified. Poirson then claimed that he had found those items.

The police also found a picture of a naked woman who was standing in the forest and looked scared among his things. They believed it was probably another one of his victims, but they were unable to identify her.

Poirson's first trial was held on September 23, 2002, for the murders of the two women he attacked at the animal cemetery, Jeanine and Monique Villain. He was convicted on both counts and sentenced to life imprisonment. His second trial was on February 2, 2005, for the murders of Lucie Pham-Ngoc-Bich and Charlotte Berson and two sexual assaults: that of Clémence and another woman, Adeline, in July 1998, the same month he was released from prison. He was again found guilty of all charges and sentenced to life imprisonment plus twenty-two years.

TWENTY-SIX

Ludivine Chambet

THE POISONER OF CHAMBÉRY

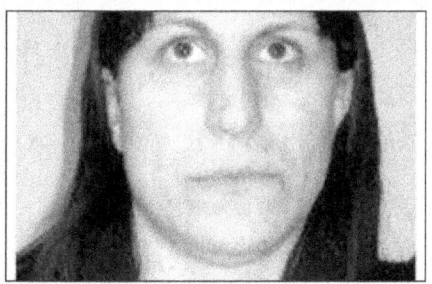

L udivine Chambet was born in France, probably in Jacob-Bellecombette, on May 10, 1983. Over the years, Chambet worked as a caregiver in several nursing homes and hospitals. She was always timid and regularly protected by her mother, so when her mother died in June 2013 from leukemia, even though Chambet was thirty at the time, she felt very alone and was never good at making friends or attending social events.

In November 2013, the same year as her mother died, one of her patients went into a coma and died soon afterward. When the hospital did an exam on the patient, they found several drugs in her bloodstream. Most were antidepressants that were not prescribed to her.

When more of the facility's patients started dying in the same manner, ten in all, suspicion ensued, and the administration began to look into the unusual deaths.

The police investigated each patient, looking into their families and histories. They also ran background checks on all the employees, including those who were always working at the time of the deaths. Chambet became one of the main suspects as soon as police realized that she was the last caretaker to see each of the patients before they died.

Within a month, police arrested Chambet and charged her with several murders by poisoning and several attempted murders also by poisoning. Once the press got the information about the crimes and who their suspect was, Chambet was dubbed "The Poisoner of Chambéry."

On May 9, 2017, Chambet's two-week trial

began. Throughout it, she would often only remember parts of her crimes, claiming that she had blacked out and couldn't recall anything. She also claimed that she never had any intentions of killing any of her patients and that she only wanted to relieve them of any pain.

On May 23rd, after only six hours of deliberation, the jury found Chambet guilty of ten murders and attempted murder by poisoning three more. She was sentenced to a twenty-five-year sentence in prison, followed by a ten-year involuntary commitment to a psychiatric ward in a hospital. She also had her medical license revoked.

TWENTY-SEVEN

David Lefèvre

THE SWAMP KILLER

David Lefèvre was born in Reims, France, on May 17, 1980. He was one of six children from parents who, according to him, were very uncaring. He claimed both of his parents physically and sexually assaulted him. When he was eight years old, Lefèvre and all his siblings were placed in a foster home. Throughout childhood, he always got into trouble by committing small thefts or crimes but nothing major until he was older.

On August 5, 1999, when Lefèvre was nineteen, he and his friend went into a department store in Laon and stole some clothing. They got away with it, making them feel confident. So, they began planning more thefts. Three days later, on August 8th, when the two friends were walking down a street, Lefèvre noticed a homeless man lying on the sidewalk. They beat the man before shooting him to death, taking what few valuables he had before fleeing the scene. Believing they had just gotten away with the murder, they began planning another robbery.

The police searched for the young men involved in the recent thefts, and Lefèvre's and his friend's names came up. After canvassing the witnesses to the murder and showing them pictures, they all identified Lefèvre as one of the culprits. On August 14th, the two were arrested, and both were charged with murder and robbery.

After their arrest, police had them analyzed by a psychiatrist, and both were deemed fit to stand trial. In June 2002, the two stood trial. The court found them guilty of all charges within three days, but because Lefèvre was only nineteen at the time of the crime, he was only sentenced to five years in prison and three years probation.

After Lefèvre was released from prison, he returned to live with his foster family. But within six months, he was arrested and jailed again for stealing a car. He was tried and convicted later that Summer and sentenced to a six-month jail term. After serving four and a half months, he was released.

The following year, in 2004, Lefèvre started to sell drugs on the streets, including cocaine. In the Spring, he was pulled over by an officer who found cocaine in his car, so he was arrested for possession. This time, when he was tried for these charges, he was sentenced to a five-year prison sentence. He was released in 2008.

After Lefèvre was released from prison this time, he moved to Amiens, where two of his friends, Julien Guerin and Sylvie T., lived. The three of them used to party and drink a lot together when they were younger in foster care, so he thought it might be fun to hang out with them again. After one year of nightlife, Guerin met seventeen-year-old Alice Caron. The two of them started dating and quickly moved in together, and soon after, they had a baby.

On January 13, 2011, Lefèvre and Guerin

decided to go out and get some cigarettes. Somehow, they ended up driving to a swamp located in Camon. Lefèvre hit Guerin over the head with a bat, causing him to lose consciousness, fall into the swamp, and drown. Lefèvre quickly left and returned home, and sometime during that drive, he disposed of the bat. The following day, Lefèvre went over to Guerin's girlfriend and told her that he dropped Guerin off in Amiens. She filed a missing person report with the police, who later questioned Lefèvre, but they had no evidence of any foul play, so he wasn't arrested.

Just over a month later, Guerin's body was discovered in the Avery River by a city employee who had been cleaning up the river bank. The coroner ruled the death as accidental because he was a known drug and alcohol addict. But the police thought the death was suspicious. The medical exam took a long time and was hard to conduct properly as his body had been in the river for a month and was severely decomposed.

That Summer, Lefèvre's other friend, Sylvie, had started dating twenty-four-year-old Alexandre Michaud. Lefèvre didn't like their relationship as it left him nobody to party with. One night in September, Sylvie got into a fight with Michaud.

He ended up punching a wall and hurt his wrist and hand. Sylvie called Lefèvre and asked him to take Michaud to the hospital for her.

After the hospital bandaged Michaud's wrist, they got into Lefèvre's car and headed home. Somehow, they ended up driving to the same swamp where Lefèvre had killed Guerin. He shot Michaud dead, leaving his body in the swamp and returning home.

Sylvie reported her missing boyfriend to the police, who began searching for him. Two days later, they discovered his body in some marshes near the river. When the police learned that Lefèvre was the last known person to have been with Michaud, and because he was a person of interest in Guerlin's suspicious death, they decided that the two cases might be connected.

Soon afterward, police wiretapped Lefèvre's apartment and put a tail on him to watch everything he did. It wasn't long before Lefèvre was heard bragging about killing three times to a friend. It was enough to bring him in for questioning, at least.

On December 11, 2011, the police brought Lefèvre in, and after several interrogations and field trips to the swampy murder scene, police charged him with the murders of Michaud and

Guerlin. Once the press got wind of him being charged and the circumstances surrounding the cases, they dubbed him the "Swamp Killer."

On March 12, 2012, Lefèvre wrote a letter to both the families and the prosecutor confessing to the murders. It included full details of how it happened and a full apology.

Lefèvre's trial started on November 12, 2013, and lasted only three days. He was convicted and then sentenced to life imprisonment without parole until December of 2033.

TWENTY-EIGHT

Nadir Sedrati

THE CANAL CUTTER

N adir Sedrati was born in Gavet, Isère, France, on March 26, 1938. He was the youngest of two boys to parents who immigrated from Algeria. When he turned three, his father died, and Nadir, along with his brother, were placed in foster care as their mother was unable to take care of them.

Nadir's older brother was kicked out of the orphanage because of his violent nature and constant fighting with the adults of the school. Nadir was allowed to stay, being the calm and quiet one of the two. The orphanage was very religious, and when he turned eight, he was baptized. Everyone called him Dominique instead of Nadir, and he grew up thinking that was his name. When he turned fourteen in 1952, he learned that his real name was Nadir, not Dominique, and that his father had died during World War II. These revelations sent him into a deep depression.

After Nadir finished school in 1957, now nineteen, he decided to join the army in his parents' country of Algeria. During his very short time in the military, he was caught running money scams and gambling. He was dishonorably discharged. Since he was only nineteen at the time, he avoided being sent to prison and instead received a fine and probation.

It wasn't long, though, before he was sent to prison. After leaving the military, he continued his fraud and theft behavior. In 1962, when he was twenty-three, he was arrested for fraud and sentenced to jail. While in prison, psychiatrists medically evaluated him. They found him sane and well enough to know the difference between right and wrong.

After his release from jail in 1968, he met and started dating a woman from Algeria. A year later, he went to meet her parents. They didn't receive Nadir very well and didn't care about his inability to speak Arabic, their native language.

Throughout the 1970s, Nadir continued his life of petty crimes and was in and out of both jail and psychiatric hospitals. During his stays at the hospitals, he claimed to be scared of space aliens he thought were coming to get him. He used to pour honey all over his body because he felt it would protect him from the aliens.

During one of his stints in jail, Nadir met and became close friends with another prisoner, André Gachy. On his release from prison in 1982, he moved to La Verriere to live with Gachy. In the Spring of that same year, they decided to go on a weekend holiday to a local resort. During that trip, Gachy disappeared.

A month later, an employee at a store in La

Rochelle noticed Nadir using Gachy's checkbook to buy items, but his identification didn't match the name on the check. The employee reported this fact to the police, and Nadir was arrested. After some further investigations by police, they realized that Gachy had been missing for over a month but were unable to find a body or any evidence of foul play.

By August of that year, the police felt that they had enough evidence to charge Nadir with murder and identity theft of Gachy. He remained in prison until his trial started three years and three months after his arrest on November 26, 1985. After four days, he was acquitted of the charges. There wasn't enough evidence to convict him and substantiate the life sentence the prosecution desired. But instead of being released from custody, the court ordered him to spend two months in a psychiatric ward for behavioral disorders. He was released on December 17th.

In October 1994, Leon Krauss, a retired sixty-two-year-old living alone in an apartment in Villeneuve-Saint-Georges, disappeared without a trace. Then suddenly, the apartment building's maintenance man got a letter, supposedly written by Krauss, informing him that he had met a woman named Colette and decided to go live with her for a while. In the meantime, the letter also claimed that he had agreed to sublet his apartment to a man named Nadir Sedrati for a while.

On Christmas Eve 1995, Nadir walked into the local police station and talked to a detective. Nadir told the detective that he was Leon Krauss, that he wanted them to contact his family on his behalf and ask them to stop bothering him, and that he didn't want to hear from them anymore.

Four months passed by before Krauss' family approached the police again. This time, they said that the letters they received from Krauss were written in a stranger's handwriting. They provided the police with a picture of the man imitating Krauss and wanted them to do something about it. One of the officers who saw the picture recognized that it was Nadir and that he had been in trouble for imitating others, so they arrested him. They tried charging Nadir with murder again, but like in the case of André Gachy, they had no body, and weren't sure there was a murder. Instead, they charged Nadir with identity theft, for which he was convicted and sentenced to five years in prison.

Nadir was released on parole in the Spring of 1999. Using one of the older fake names he had used years before, he purchased cyanide. After that, he rented a room from a man, Jean Stauffer, in the town of Nancy under a different name, Phillippe Grissiord. Nadir then contacted one of his old cellmates, Gérard Steil, who had also recently been released. He contacted him using his new fake name and offered Steil a job if he traveled to Nancy.

On May 19th, Steil told his family that he was taking a job in Nancy, then boarded the train. Once he arrived in Nancy, he was greeted by Nadir, whom he recognized immediately as his old cellmate. The two returned to Nadir's apartment for a drink and to talk. Nadir dropped the cyanide into Steil's drink without him realizing it, and after he finished the drink, he died.

Nadir then dismembered his body, packed the pieces into his car, and dropped them in the canal. He returned to his apartment and cleaned up the mess from cutting up Steil's body.

A few days later, Nadir contacted another of his old cellmates from prison, Hans Gassen, and invited him to his apartment to discuss a possible job. Once Gassen arrived, Nadir offered him a drink. Once again, the drink was poisoned with cyanide, and after Gassen drank it, he died. Nadir then dismembered Gassen's body and dumped his remains into the canal as well. When Gassen didn't return home for a few days, his family reported him missing to the police.

A few weeks later, on May 30th, a man was fishing on the canal in Nancy when he discovered a human foot. He called the police. The following day, a rotted head was also found close to where the foot was found in the canal. Police then decided to do a thorough check on the canal, and several other body parts were discovered, including a hand, sternum, some ribs, and a left foot.

Upon medical examination of the body parts found, it was concluded that they had all been cut or surgically removed, suggesting this was a murder case. Because of the amount of decomposition from being in the water for so long, they could not get any fingerprints from the hand. But in July, after the hand was sent for analysis in Paris, it was identified as belonging to Hans Glassen, an ex-con who had just been released from prison within the last year.

When detectives talked to Glassen's roommate, they learned he was to meet a man in Nancy about a business proposition. After searching the phone records, they saw that Glassen had received several phone calls from an apartment in Nancy belonging to Phillippe Grossiord.

Nadir realized that police were on his trail. So, he answered an ad from a man looking to buy a used camper, telling him he had one to sell. The two men met, and Nadir beat the man to death, crushed his head in a blade grinder, and then dumped it in an unknown place, which had never been found.

On July 23rd, Nadir was arrested and charged with the murder of Hans Glassen. Upon further investigation, they discovered Nadir knew Gérard Steil as well, and that he was also missing. Believing that the other body parts might belong to Steil, they asked for some DNA samples from his family members to test. It was soon proven to be a positive match to one of the body parts.

Nadir's trial began on April 25, 2002, and was held in the Meurthe-et-Moselle. Even though Nadir claimed to be innocent on all charges throughout the trial, the tone changed in court once evidence was revealed that police found the blood of the victims in his apartment sink.

On May 3, 2003, over a year after the trial began, Nadir was found guilty on all counts and sentenced to life imprisonment. He wasn't long appealing the verdict.

A year later, the appeal was heard at the court in Metz. Again, Nadir was found guilty of all charges. Nadir filed another appeal, but the Court of Cassation rejected it on October 7, 2004.

Nadir Sedrati is still in prison but has been eligible for parole since 2021.

Sources

1. gallica.bnf.fr/ark:/12148/bpt6k77016g.pdf
2. Deloux, Jean-Pierre, Vacher l'éventreur, E/dite Histoire, 2000
3. Kershaw, Alister: *Murder in France*, Constable, London, 1955
4. Starr, Douglas: *The Killer of Little Shepherds: A True Crime Story and the Birth of Forensic Science*. Alfred A. Knopf, New York, 2010, ISBN 978-0-307-26619-4
5. 104705026.pdf (*nytimes.com*)
6. "Black Widows: Veiled in Their Own Web of Darkness," The Crime Library
7. Jeanne Weber, the Ogress of the Goutte d'Or - 28 rue Affre (eklablog.com)
8. Le Droit December 24, 1914 - (December 24-1914) | *RetroNews* - The BnF press site
9. L'Écho d'Alger 27 July 1914 - (27-July-1914) | *RetroNews* - The BnF press site
10. Le Petit Marseillais 17 December 1907 - (17-December-1907) | *RetroNews* - The BnF press site
11. Le Petit Provençal 14 November 1913 - (14-November-1913) | *RetroNews* - The BnF press site
12. L'Ouest-Éclair August 22, 1916 - (Aug. 22, 1916) | *RetroNews* - The BnF press site
13. Le Matin 25 July 1916 - (25-July-1916) | *RetroNews* - The BnF press si

14. The Lightning West January 20, 1916 - (January 20, 1916) | *RetroNews* - The BnF press site
15. L'Ouest-Éclair January 3, 1916 - (January 3-1916) | *RetroNews* - The BnF press site
16. The Lightning West January 19, 1916 - (January 19-1916) | *RetroNews* - The BnF press site
17. The Lightning West January 16, 1916 - (January 16-1916) | *RetroNews* - The BnF press site
18. L'Ouest-Éclair 26 July 1916 - (26-July-1916) | *RetroNews* - The BnF press site
19. L'Ouest-Éclair 26 July 1916 - (26-July-1916) | *RetroNews* - The BnF press site
20. Bardens, Dennis: *The Ladykiller: The Crimes of Landru, the French Bluebeard*, P. Davies, London, 1972.
21. Belin, J.: *Commissaire Belin*. Trente Ans de Sûreté Nationale, Bibliothèque FranceSoir, Paris, 1950.
22. Smith, Jo Durden: *100 Most Infamous Criminals*, 2004, ISBN 0-7607-4849-7
23. Newton, Michael. "Dr. Marcel Petiot," crimelibrary.com
24. King, David: *Death in the City of Light*, 2011, ISBN: 978-0-307-45289-4
25. https://www.retronews.fr/journal/le-temps/9-decembre-1934/123/649815/3
26. https://www.retronews.fr/journal/le-populaire/8-decembre-1934/110/1189579/1
27. https://gallica.bnf.fr/ark:/12148/bpt6k628300t
28. https://www.retronews.fr/journal/excelsior/7-novembre-1935/353/2773791/1
29. https://www.retronews.fr/journal/le-petit-provencal/18-fevrier-1936/677/2988101/5

30. https://www.retronews.fr/journal/le-petit-journal/6-novembre-1935/100/407255/5
31. Le Petit Journal, May 20, 1936, *RetroNews*, The BnF press site
32. L'Écho de Paris, 25 November 1935, *RetroNews*, The BnF press site
33. Flanner, Janet: *Paris was Yesterday*, 1972, The Viking Press
34. Claude Cancès: *History of 36 quai des Orfèvres*, 28 March 2019, ISBN: 978-2-37254-126-8
35. https://referentiel.nouvelobs.com/archives_pdf/OBS0617_19760906/OBS0617_19760906_042.pdf
36. https://www.lemonde.fr/archives/article/1982/06/18/aux-assises-du-val-d-oise-bernard-pesquet-par-lui-meme_3108751_1819218.html
37. "Bring in the accused: Albert Millet, the man who killed the woman who said no to him" (bfmtv.com)
38. "Release denied for Tommy Recco, 83, one of the oldest prisons in France" (lepoint.fr)
39. "Béziers: Thomy Recco's conditional release examined this Friday," (midilibre.fr)
40. Tommy Recco case: "If my wife's murderer gets out of prison, I'm ready for anything" (newsrnd.com)
41. Death sentences (*free.fr*)
42. "Death penalty. Those condemned who narrowly escaped execution 40 years ago in France" (dna.fr)
43. Michel Peiry: "The Sadist of Romont," Murders of All Kinds (over-blog.com)

44. "KILLER SIX TIMES 'YES, I LIKE KILLING'," the Repubblica.it

45. "Succo the ice-eyed killer who terrorized Mestre and France," (ilgazzettino.it)

46. "Arrest reported in 21 slayings," *The Globe and Mail*, December 4, 1987

47. "Death sentence", *The Independent*, March 23, 1989

48. "Accomplice of Old Ladies' Killer Freed," POLICEtcetera (lemonde.fr)

49. INFO FRANCEINFO. "Serial killer Francis Heaulme was indicted again for a murder committed in 1989" (francetvinfo.fr)

50. "Former police officer confesses he is notorious French serial killer Le Grêlé in suicide note" (thetimes.co.uk)

51. "French ex-officers' DNA ends 35-year murder hunt" (bbc.com)

52. "TESTIMONY: in La Grande-Motte, the neighbors of François Vérove, the serial killer known as "the Hail," are stunned" (francetvinfo.fr)

53. "The Fourniret couple have divorced," Le Parisien

54. "Kidnapped at the age of 13 by Fourniret-L'Avenir" (lavenir.net)

55. "Serial killer Michel Fourniret confessed to the murders of two women" Libération

56. "Mulhouse. He accused himself of about thirty crimes" ladepeche.fr

57. "Indicted of two accomplices of the "killer of the old ladies" Le Parisien

58. "Keller hangs himself after accusing himself of thirty murders" (lefigaro.fr)
59. "Trial of a man who hated men. Rémy Roy killed three homosexuals, including the mage Nathaniel, recruited via the pink Minitel" Liberation web.archive.org/web/20180628125020/http://www.liberation.fr/france-archive/1996/06/28/federation=archive.wikiwix.com
60. "The man who hated men denies killing Claude Roy, 33, has appeared since Friday before the Val-de-Marne Assize Court" Liberation
61. "Honoré Zanchi sentenced on appeal to thirty years in prison" France Bleu
62. "Drôme: Verdict in the trial of Honoré Zanchi" (francetvinfo.fr)
63. "Mysterious biker murders solved in Drôme-Ardèche" Le Parisien
64. "First trial of the serial killer stonemason" Le Parisien
65. "New trial for the killer of old ladies" Le Parisien
66. "Nadir Sedrati | Nadir Sédrati: many faces" L'Est Républicain
67. "In Nancy, the same suspect for the corpses of the canal. Many details converge on a man already imprisoned," Liberation
68. "Experts consider Nadir Sedrati extremely dangerous" Le Parisien
69. "The human remains to denounce their butcher. A new indictment in the case of the murders of the Rhine-Marne canal," Liberation
70. "13 older adults poisoned: the nursing assistant sentenced to 25 years" lindependant.fr

71. "Chambéry: who is the nursing assistant suspected of poisoning?" (nouvelobs.com)
72. "At the Chambéry trial, the mysteries of the caregiver Ludivine Chambet" (la-croix.com)
73. "Murders in Essonne: Yoni Palmier sentenced to life in prison on appeal" (lemonde.fr)
74. "Double murder near Amiens: the accused sentenced to life imprisonment" (20minutes.fr)
75. "Double murder near Amiens: the accused sentenced to life imprisonment" (20minutes.fr)

About the Author

Alan R Warren is a
Bestselling Author,
Producer, and host of the
popular NBC Radioshow
House of Mystery and *Inside
Writing,* both heard on the
106.5 F.M. Los
Angeles/102.3 F.M.
Riverside/ 1050 A.M.
Palm Springs/ 540 A.M.
KYAH Salt Lake City/

1150 A.M. KKNW Seattle/Tacoma and Phoenix.
His bestselling true crime books in Canada
include *Beyond Suspicion: The True Story of Colonel
Russell Williams,* which will be featured on CNN's
Lies, Crimes, & Videos (Season 4), and *Murder Times
Six: The True Story of the Wells Gray Park Murders.* In
America, his bestsellers include *The Killing Game:
Serial Killer Rodney Alcala,* which was featured on

several television shows such as *Very Scary People with Donny Walberg*, Oxygen's *Mark of a Killer*, Reelz' *Killer Trophies*, and soon to be included in a four-part Sundance Channel documentary called *Death's Date*. His bestseller, *Doomsday Cults: The Devil's Hostages*, was featured on Vice's *Dark Side of the '90s*.

His latest series, *Killer Queens*, is a six-part book series covering murders that affect the Gay Community. So far, it includes Book 1 - Leopold & Loeb, Book 2 - Butcher of Hanover: Fritz Haarmann, Book 3 - Grindr Serial Killer: Stephen Port, and Book 4 - Bruce McArthur: Toronto Gay Killer.

Also By Alan R. Warren

Murderous Minds – Germany

The *International Serial Killers Encyclopedia* series sheds light on the murderous minds of many killers, including their motivations, methods, and madness, through detailed research and explicit retelling of events. Some are notorious names that echo through history books, while others are lesser-known killers whose stories are no less harrowing. Each volume reveals a new layer of darkness.

Volume 1 of the series focuses on the most notorious serial killers from Germany. It contains many cases where the twisted minds and deeds of those who stalked the streets of Germany left a trail of fear and destruction in their wake.

From the infamous Fritz Haarmann, a.k.a. the "Butcher of Hanover," who preyed upon young boys with chilling brutality, to Peter Kürten, a.k.a. the "Vampire of Dusseldorf," whose thirst for blood knew no bounds.

Each chapter reveals the brutal tales of individuals consumed by their darkest desires and a compelling blend of true crime and psychological intrigue.

Murderous Minds Germany offers a chilling glimpse into the darkest recesses of the human psyche, reminding us that evil can lurk just beneath the surface, even in the most civilized society.

Murderous Minds – Soviet Union

The *International Serial Killers Encyclopedia* series sheds light on the murderous minds of many killers, including their motivations, methods, and madness, through detailed research and explicit retelling of events. Some are notorious names that echo through history books, while others are lesser-known killers whose stories are no less harrowing. Each volume reveals a new layer of darkness.

Volume 2 of the series focuses on the most notorious serial killers from the Soviet Union Era of history. In the shadows of the Iron Curtain, amidst the turmoil of revolution and the rigid structures of the Soviet regime, a different kind of darkness lurked. Behind closed doors and beneath the watchful eyes of the state, a breed of killers emerged, their crimes shrouded in secrecy and fear from the haunting corridors of Moscow to the desolate landscapes of Siberia.

From Andrei Chikatilo, a.k.a. the "Butcher of Rostov," whose insatiable hunger for violence claimed the lives of dozens, leaving a trail of mutilation and terror in his wake, to Vasili Komaroff, a.k.a. the "Wolf of Moscow," who killed so many men, he couldn't even remember his kill count. Each chapter reveals the brutal tales of individuals consumed by their darkest desires and a compelling blend of true crime and psychological intrigue.

Murderous Minds Soviet Union delves deeper, revealing the many enigmatic figures who haunted a nation's collective consciousness. Each chapter unveils a new layer of horror and intrigue where the echoes of the past continue to reverberate to this day.

MURDER TIMES SIX: The True Story of The Wells Park Murders

"The author even had me (who conducted the interview) on the edge of my seat as I was turning the pages as "the Detective" was trying to unearth the unspeakable truth."

It was a crime unlike anything seen in British Columbia. The horror of the "Wells Gray Murders" almost forty years ago transcends decades.

On August 2, 1982, three generations of a family set out on a camping trip – Bob and Jackie Johnson, their two daughters, Janet, 13 and Karen, 11, and Jackie's parents, George and Edith Bentley. A month later, the Johnson family car was found off a mountainside logging road near Wells Gray Park completely burned out. In the back seat were the incinerated remains of four adults, and in the trunk were the two girls.

But this was not just your average mass murder. It was much worse. Over time, some brutal details were revealed; however, most are still only known to the murderer, David Ennis (formerly Shearing). His crimes had far-reaching impacts on the family, community, and country. It still does today. Every time Shearing attempts freedom from the parole board, the grief is triggered as everyone is forced to relive the horrors once again.

Murder Times Six shines a spotlight on the crime that

captured the attention of a nation, recounts the narrative of a complex police investigation, and discusses whether a convicted mass murderer should ever be allowed to leave the confines of an institution. Most importantly, it tells the story of one family forever changed.

Beyond Suspicion: Russell Williams – A Canadian Serial Killer

Young girl's panties started to go missing; sexual assaults began to occur, and then female bodies were found! Soon this quiet town of Tweed, Ontario, was in a panic. What is even more shocking was when an upstanding resident stood accused of the assaults. This was not just any man, but a pillar of the community; a decorated military pilot who had flown Canadian Forces VIP aircraft for dignitaries such as the Queen of England, Prince Philip, the Governor-General and Prime Minister of Canada.

This is the story of serial killer Russell Williams, the elite pilot of Canada's Air Force One, and the innocent victims he murdered. Unlike other serial killers, Williams seemed very unaffected about his crimes and leading two different lives.

Alan R. Warren describes the secret life including the abductions, rape, and murders that were unleashed on an unsuspecting community. Included are letters written to the victims by Williams and descriptions of the assaults and rapes as seen on videos and photos taken by Williams during the attacks.

This updated version also contains the full brilliant police interrogation of Williams and his confession. Also, the twisted way the Williams planned to pin his crimes on his unsuspecting neighbor.

Doomsday Cults: The Devil's Hostages

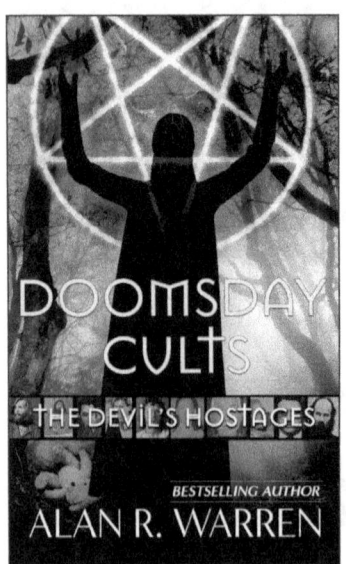

Jim Jones convinced his 1000 followers they would all have to commit suicide since he was going to die. Shoko Asahara convinced his followers to release a weapon of mass destruction, the deadly sarin gas, on a Tokyo subway. The Order of the Solar Temple lured the rich and famous, including Princess Grace of Monaco, and convinced them to die a fiery death now on Earth to be reborn on a better planet called Sirius. Charles Manson convinced his followers to kill, in an attempt to incite an apocalyptic race war.

These are a few of the doomsday cults examined in this book by bestselling author Alan R. Warren. Its focus is on cults whose destructive behavior was due in large part to their apocalyptic beliefs or doomsday movements. It includes details surrounding the massacres and a look into how their members became so brainwashed they committed unimaginable crimes at the command of their leader.

Usually, when we hear about these cults and their massacres, we ask ourselves how it possibly happened. We could also ask ourselves, what then is the difference between a cult and a religion? We once had a small group of people who unquestionably followed a person who believed he was the son of God. Two thousand years later, that following is one of the most recognized religions in the world. This book in no way criticizes believing in God. Rather, it examines how a social movement grows into a full religion and when it does not. And what makes the conventional faiths such as Christianity, Judaism, Islam, and Hinduism stand above groups such as the Branch Davidians or Children of God.

In Chains: The Dangerous World of Human Trafficking

Human trafficking is the trade of people for forced labor or sex. It also includes the illegal extraction of human organs and tissues. And it is an extremely ruthless and dangerous industry plaguing our world today.

Most believe human trafficking occurs in countries with no human rights legislation. This is a myth. All types of human trafficking are alive and well in most of the developed countries of the world, like the United States, Canada, and the UK. It is estimated that $150 billion a year is generated in the forced labor industry alone. It is also believed that 21 million people are trapped in modern-day slavery – exploited for sex, labor, or organs.

Most also believe since they live in a free country, there is built-in protection against such illegal practices. But for many, this is not the case. Traffickers tend to focus on the most vulnerable in our society, but trafficking can happen to anyone. You will see how easy it can happen in the stories included in "In Chains."

BUTCHER OF HANOVER: Fritz Haarmann (Killer Queens 2)

Killer Queens is a new series of historical fiction books based on true stories. Sources, such as police reports and newspaper articles, are examined to gather as many facts as possible surrounding each case. As with any work of fiction, some creative additions are made when telling these stories, usually within the conversations between the personalities between the personalities involved. The various sources are the basis of these conversations and hopefully, make them come alive for the readers to help understand what was meant by those words.

Book 2 of the series focuses on the serial killer of at least twenty-seven young men and boys in Germany in the post-World War I era. At the center of this murder case were Fritz Haarmann and Hans Grans, who were lovers while committing these murders. It wasn't until the skulls and bones started washing ashore from the Leine River in Hanover that Germany realized they had a cold-blooded serial killer in their country.

Unlike Leopold and Loeb murder case covered in Book 1, where the dominance shifted from one to the other,

Fritz Haarmann was the dominant partner in this case. He carried out each of the murders and dismemberment of the bodies himself, even though he claimed that Grans chose who was to be murdered in court.

As you read the exploration of the case in this book, ask yourself, did Haarmann murder each victim to keep his lover Hans Grans to stay with him? Did Grans decide who it was that was to be murdered? The evidence on this case will keep you on the edge of your seat, trying to determine who was really behind these gruesome murders.

www.ingramcontent.com/pod-product-compliance
Lightning Source LLC
Chambersburg PA
CBHW070921120626
46546CB00001B/348